Santiago Calatrava

Philip Jodidio

TASCHEN

KÖLN LONDON MADRID NEW YORK PARIS TOKYO

Calatrava

Agradecimiento > Ringraziamenti > Agradecimentos

El editor y el autor desean agradecer a
Robertina Calatrava y a Kim Marangoni
su amable ayuda en la realización de
este libro.

L'editore e l'autore desiderano ringraziare
Robertina Calatrava e Kim Marangoni per
la gentile assistenza nella preparazione
di questo libro.

O editor e o autor agradecem a Robertina
Calatrava e a Kim Marangoni pelo seu
gentil apoio durante a preparação deste
livro.

Página 1 > Pagina 1 > Página 1
Portrait Santiago Calatrava, 1997
Photo: Luca Vignelli (Nueva York)

Página 2 > Pagina 2 > Página 2
Trinity Bridge, Salford, England (1993-1995)
Photo: J.E. Linden

© 2001 Taschen GmbH
Hohenzollernring 53, D–50672 Köln
www.taschen.com

Edited by Angela Pfotenhauer, Cologne
Design: Quim Nolla, [di´zain], Barcelona
Spanish translation: José García, Cologne
Italian translation: Doriana Comerlati, Milan
Portuguese translation: Carla de Sousa,
Lisbon

Printed in Spain
ISBN 3-8228-5614-2

Indice > **Sommario** > Índice

Santiago Calatrava es, por diversos conceptos, un personaje fuera de lo común. Nació cerca de Valencia, en 1951, y en la ciudad del Turia estudió Arte antes de iniciar la carrera de Arquitectura en la misma capital levantina. Pero más insólito aún es que, después de finalizarla, se decidiera a seguir estudios de Ingeniería Civil en la Universidad Técnica Helvética (ETH) de Zúrich. Allí se doctoró, en el año 1981, con una tesis titulada «Sobre la plegabilidad de las cerchas». En una época en que un buen número de arquitectos famosos no dudan en declararse autodidactas, la formación de Calatrava no podría ser más académica. No sólo habla con total fluidez español, inglés, francés y alemán, sino que también sobrepasa las barreras entre el arte, la arquitectura y la ingeniería con la misma facilidad con que cruza las fronteras entre los países. Santiago Calatrava se ha convertido así en una de las figuras más importantes de nuestro tiempo, en uno de los jefes de fila de la generación que ha comenzado a dominar la arquitectura mundial. La casa que le sirve tanto de residencia como de estudio, en las proximidades del Lago de Zúrich, revela buena parte del carácter y del proceso de trabajo propios de Santiago Calatrava. Este sólido edificio de piedra podría ser calificado de burgués si se observa tan sólo desde el exterior, a pesar de que sobre el césped se encuentra un buen número de esculturas de Calatrava. Pero en el interior, el arquitecto ha remodelado completamente el edificio, dándole un aspecto moderno y diáfano, que no consiguen perturbar ni los objetos extraños ni el desorden. Fácilmente podría suponerse que éste es el estudio, no de un arquitecto o ingeniero, sino de un escultor o pintor: prácticamente no se ven planos, ni siquiera maquetas; por el contrario se tropieza a cada paso con las esculturas, los dibujos, el mobiliario y las lámparas de Calatrava. La relación entre las obras artísticas de Calatrava y sus proyectos arquitectónicos es compleja, aun cuando algunas formas, como la de la Estación del TGV en Lyón-Satolas —ese edificio similar a un inmenso pájaro prehistórico—, puedan reconocerse sin dificultad en sus esculturas. «A veces, me dedico a hacer composiciones

Santiago Calatrava è sotto molti aspetti una figura fuori del comune. Nato in Spagna nel 1951, ha studiato arte e successivamente architettura a Valencia. Cosa più singolare, ha poi proseguito gli studi a Zurigo nell'ambito dell'ingegneria civile, frequentando il Politecnico federale svizzero (ETH) e conseguendovi nel 1981 il dottorato con una tesi sul tema «Piegabilità delle strutture». In tempi in cui più di un architetto famoso non esita a proclamarsi autodidatta, la formazione di Calatrava è, al contrario, brillantemente accademica. Parla spagnolo, inglese, francese e tedesco quasi con la stessa scioltezza; valica le barriere tra l'arte, l'architettura e l'ingegneria con la medesima facilità con cui cambia paese: Calatrava è evidentemente una figura con cui oggi bisogna fare i conti, uno dei principali esponenti di una generazione che incomincia a dominare l'architettura internazionale. La casa sulle rive del lago di Zurigo che gli serve sia da abitazione che da studio rivela molto del suo carattere e del suo metodo di lavoro. Vista dall'esterno, questa solida costruzione in pietra non può che essere descritta come borghese, malgrado la presenza delle sculture di Calatrava disposte sul prato circostante. Internamente, però, l'architetto ha completamente trasformato la struttura dell'edificio e gli ha conferito un aspetto essenziale e moderno, che non viene turbato da oggetti estranei o dal disordine. Un visitatore non informato potrebbe farsi l'opinione che si tratta della casa-studio di uno scultore o di un pittore, piuttosto che di un architetto o un ingegnere. Disegni tecnici o modelli architettonici sono a malapena visibili, mentre sono onnipresenti sculture, disegni, mobili e lampade creati da Calatrava. Il rapporto tra le sue opere d'arte e le sue realizzazioni architettoniche è complesso, anche se alcune forme, come quella della stazione per i TGV di Lione-Satolas che richiama la silhouette di un uccello, sono subito identificabili nelle sue sculture. «Talvolta creo delle composizioni strutturali che, se

Santiago Calatrava é, sob muitos aspectos, uma figura invulgar. Tendo nascido em Espanha no ano de 1951, estudou arte e arquitectura em Valência. Inesperadamente, partiu então para Zurique a fim de estudar engenharia civil no Instituto Federal de Tecnologia Suíço(ETH). Em 1981, completa aí o seu doutoramento com a tese «Encurvamento de Estruturas Tridimensionais». Numa época em que alguns arquitectos ilustres não hesitam em proclamar o seu carácter autodidáctico, a formação de Calatrava é, pelo contrário, de base académica. Santiago Calatrava, que fala quase com a mesma fluência o espanhol, o inglês, o francês e o alemão, permitindo-lhe extrapolar as fronteiras entre a arte, a arquitectura e a engenharia com a facilidade com que muda de país, é um personagem que não devemos descurar, o farol de uma geração que começa agora a dominar a arquitectura internacional.

A casa à beira do lago que possui em Zurique, que é, ao mesmo tempo, a residência e o escritório de Santiago Calatrava, revela o seu carácter e o seu processo de trabalho. Esta construção em pedra maciça poderá ser considerada vulgar quando observada do exterior, apesar das esculturas de Calatrava dispersas pelo relvado. Contudo, o arquitecto remodelou completamente a estrutura interior, concedendo-lhe um aspecto limpo e moderno, apenas turbado por alguns objectos estranhos e uma ligeira desordem. Um visitante mal informado não julgará tratar-se do local de trabalho de um arquitecto ou de um engenheiro, mas de um pintor ou de um escultor. Estão expostas poucas ou nenhumas maquetas arquitectónicas, enquanto que as suas esculturas, desenhos, mobiliário e candeeiros encontram-se omnipresentes.

A relação entre as obras artísticas de Calatrava e os seus projectos arquitectónicos é complexa, mesmo se algumas formas, como é o caso da estação de TGV de Lyon-Satolas, com a configuração de um pássaro, sejam de certo modo identificáveis com as suas esculturas. «Por vezes, crio composições estruturais, as quais poderão denominar esculturas, se assim o entenderem», diz Calatrava. «São baseadas em ideias muito pessoais. Da mesma maneira que Fellini ou Kurosawa desenhavam esboços antes dos seus filmes, eu faço esculturas.» Calatrava faz referências frequentes à arte, a qual é certamente uma das chaves da sua obra, como se pode deduzir da observação da sua casa em Zurique. «Concebi uma série de pontes com arcos inclinados que poderá ser comparada àquela dos Banhistas de Cézanne», observa. «A arte deste século tem sido profundamente influenciada pelo conceito marxista-leninista da arte para todos. Agora, já nada disso existe. Reencontrámos enfim a liberdade para criar, o que significa uma nova posição para o arquitecto enquanto artista, e para a arquitectura enquanto arte.»[1]

Calatrava não parece muito preocupado com os papéis respectivos do arquitecto e do engenheiro no processo de construção, ou mesmo na sua própria pesquisa. «Em princípio», refere, «o arquitecto é o responsável, e o engenheiro trabalha para ele.» No entanto, o seu interesse alternado em arte,

estructurales; si se quiere, también se pueden denominar esculturas», dice Santiago Calatrava. «Se basan en ideas muy personales. Al igual que Fellini o Kurosawa hacían dibujos antes de comenzar a rodar sus filmes, yo hago esculturas». Las frecuentes referencias de Santiago Calatrava al arte es, indudablemente, una de las claves para comprender su obra. «Una serie de puentes que he proyectado, con arcos inclinados, quizá podría compararse con la serie de 'bañistas' de Cézanne», declara. «El arte del siglo XX — continúa— se ha visto fuertemente influenciado por el concepto marxista-leninista del arte para todos. Esta idea se ha pasado ya. Estamos volviendo a encontrar la libertad de creación, lo que implica un nuevo puesto para el arquitecto en tanto artista, y para la arquitectura en tanto arte.»[1]

Santiago Calatrava no parece especialmente preocupado por los respectivos papeles que han de desempeñar la arquitectura y la ingeniería en el proceso de la construcción, o incluso en sus propias obras. «En principio, el arquitecto es el responsable; el ingeniero trabaja para él», dice al respecto. Sin embargo, debido al interés que simultáneamente manifiesta por el arte, la ingeniería y la arquitectura, Calatrava se encuentra en el foco de uno de los más intensos debates en la historia reciente de la construcción y del diseño. Como dijo Sigfried Giedion en su gran obra *Espacio, tiempo y arquitectura*: «El advenimiento del ingeniero especialista con una mayor rapidez en el manejo de los elementos industrializados amenazó la posición privilegiada del arquitecto y sentó las bases para los desarrollos actuales. El ingeniero del siglo XIX asumió inconscientemente el papel de guía de esos nuevos elementos que facilitó continuamente al arquitecto. Desarrolló formas anónimas y universales al mismo tiempo.» Giedion reconstruye el debate en torno al papel del ingeniero aludiendo a una serie de fechas y acontecimientos esenciales. Entre éstas cabe citar «1877: En aquel año, el problema fue llevado a la Academia, la cual ofreció un premio al mejor trabajo que versara sobre 'La unión o la separación del ingeniero y del arquitecto'. Davioud, uno de los arquitectos que

vuole, può anche chiamare sculture», spiega Santiago Calatrava. «Si basano su idee molto personali. Fellini o Kurosawa facevano dei disegni prima di passare ai film. Ecco, io invece creo delle sculture.» L'architetto fa frequenti riferimenti all'arte, che è senza dubbio una delle chiavi di lettura del suo lavoro, come risulta subito evidente dalla sua casa di Zurigo. «Ho progettato una serie di ponti ad archi inclinati che potrebbe essere paragonata alla serie delle *Bagnanti* di Cézanne», osserva Calatrava. «L'arte del XX secolo è stata pesantemente influenzata dal concetto marxista-leninista dell'arte per tutti. Oggi non è più così. Adesso ritroviamo la libertà di creare, e ciò implica un nuovo posto per l'architetto come artista, e per l'architettura come arte.»[1]

Calatrava non sembra farsi un problema dei rispettivi ruoli dell'architettura e dell'ingegneria nell'ambito dell'edilizia, nemmeno per quanto riguarda il suo stesso lavoro. «Sostanzialmente», afferma, «l'architetto è responsabile e l'ingegnere lavora per lui.» E tuttavia, con i suoi interessi che spaziano dall'arte all'ingegneria all'architettura, Calatrava si ritrova proprio nel cuore di uno dei dibattiti più infuocati della storia recente della costruzione e della progettazione. Come ha scritto Sigfried Giedion nel suo fondamentale *Spazio, tempo e architettura*, «l'avvento dell'ingegnere strutturale e di tecniche costruttive industrializzate più rapide e portatrici di forme ha messo fine alla posizione privilegiata dell'architetto e posto le basi degli sviluppi attuali. L'ingegnere del XIX secolo ha assunto inconsciamente il ruolo di guardiano degli elementi innovativi che via via forniva all'architetto. Sviluppava forme che erano al tempo stesso anonime e universali». Giedion ricostruisce il dibattito sul ruolo dell'ingegneria citando una serie di date ed eventi essenziali. Fra questi: «1877: quell'anno il problema fece il suo ingresso all'Accademia, quando venne offerto un premio per la migliore relazione sul tema dell'"unione o separazione tra ingegnere e architetto". Davioud, uno degli architetti del Trocadéro, vinse il premio con questa risposta: "Non ci sarà un accordo vero,

engenharia e arquitectura coloca-o no centro de um dos debates mais acesos na história recente da construção e da concepção. Como escreveu Sigfried Giedion na sua obra maior, *Space, Time and Architecture*, «A chegada do engenheiro especializado à área da estrutura, armado de técnicas mais rápidas e industrializadas doque as pesquisas convencionais, provocou o ênfase artístico, salientou a posição privilegiada do arquitecto e proporcionou uma nova base para o progresso actual. O engenheiro do século XIX adoptou inconscientemente o papel de guardião dos novos elementos que, de forma contínua, apresentava aos arquitectos. Estavam então em desenvolvimento formas que eram, ao mesmo tempo, anónimas e universais.» Giedion reevoca a origem do debate sobre a função da engenharia citando algumas datas essenciais. Entre elas, «1877: neste ano, a questão surgiu na Academia quando foi proposto um prémio para a melhor dissertação sobre o tema da união ou separação entre o arquitecto e o engenheiro. Davioud, um dos arquitectos do Trocadéro, arrebatou o galardão com a seguinte resposta: «O pacto nunca se tornará realidade, completo e frutífero até que o engenheiro, o artista e o cientista se fundam numa só pessoa. Durante um longo período, vivemos com a absurda convicção de que a arte era um género de actividade distinto de todas as outras manifestações de inteligência humana, tendo como única fonte e origem a personalidade do próprio artista e a sua imaginação caprichosa.»[2] Ainda que nem a insistência de Giedion no «anonimato» nem a referência de Davioud à «imaginação caprichosa» do artista combinem com a poderosa originalidade de Calatrava, este poderá materializar actualmente a profecia do arquitecto francês sobre o pacto entre o engenheiro e o arquitecto.

A HERANÇA DOS ENGENHEIROS E DOS ARTISTAS

O catálogo da exposição de 1993 de Calatrava no Museum of Modern Art de Nova Iorque sublinha a estreita ligação entre a sua obra e aquela de outros engenheiros precursores: «Calatrava pertence ao património mais notável da engenharia do século XX. Como os grandes mestres das gerações precedentes – Robert Maillart, Pier Luigi Nervi, Eduardo Torroja e Félix Candela – Calatrava supera a aproximação direccionada para a mera resolução de problemas técnicos. Para esses engenheiros, a estrutura resulta de um equilíbrio entre o critério científico de eficácia e a inovação no âmbito da pesquisa formal. Calatrava considera a engenharia como "a arte do possível", e procura um novo vocabulário formal baseado no conhecimento tecnológico, não sendo, porém, uma ode à técnica.»[3] O primeiro citado, Robert Maillart (1872–1940), diplomado pelo ETH de Zurique em 1894, produziu algumas das pontes mais espectaculares da época moderna, e empregou o betão de maneira inovadora. O seu entreposto de Giesshübel em Zurique (1910) recorreu pela primeira vez a um tecto de betão em forma de cogumelo, o que lhe permitiu dispensar o uso de vigas. Como Matilda McQuaid escreve, «Maillart foi um dos primeiros engenheiros deste século a romper completamente

< Campo Volantin Footbridge, Bilbao, Spain
> Bach de Roda–Felipe II, Barcelona, Spain

proyectaron el Trocadéro, se llevó el premio con esta respuesta: 'El acorde no llegará nunca a ser real, completo y fructífero hasta el día en que el ingeniero, el artista y el hombre de ciencia estén fundidos en una misma persona. Durante mucho tiempo hemos vivido dominados por la disparatada idea de que el arte era una forma de actividad distinta de todas las restantes actividades de la inteligencia humana, teniendo su única fuente y origen en la personalidad del propio artista y, en ella, su caprichosa fantasía»[2] Aun cuando ni la insistencia de Giedion en el «anonimato» del trabajo del ingeniero ni la referencia de Davioud a los «caprichos de la imaginación» del artista pueden avenirse con la pujante originalidad de Calatrava, éste bien parece materializar los requerimientos del arquitecto francés de armonizar la ingeniería y la arquitectura.

LA HERENCIA DE LOS INGENIEROS Y LOS ARTISTAS

El catálogo de la exposición de Calatrava que en 1993 organizó el Museum of Modern Art de Nueva York subraya la estrecha relación que existe entre sus obras y las de otros grandes pioneros de la ingeniería: «Calatrava forma parte del patrimonio más destacado de la ingeniería del siglo XX. Como los representantes de la generación precedente —Robert Maillart, Pier Luigi Nervi, Eduardo Torroja y Félix Candela—, Calatrava no se contenta tan sólo con solucionar problemas técnicos. Para esos ingenieros, una construcción es el equilibrio entre el criterio científico de la eficiencia y la innovación formal. Calatrava considera la ingeniería como 'el arte de lo factible'; busca un nuevo lenguaje formal basado en los conocimientos técnicos, que sin embargo no es un himno a la técnica.»[3] El primero de los ingenieros citados, Robert Maillart (1872–1940) se graduó en la ETH de Zúrich en 1894 y construyó algunos de los puentes modernos más espectaculares, con un uso realmente innovador del hormigón. Para sus almacenes Giesshübel (Zúrich, 1910) empleó por primera vez una estructura de hormigón fungiforme para resolver el techo, lo que le permitía renunciar al uso de vigas.

completo e fruttuoso fino a quando l'ingegnere, l'artista e lo scienziato non si fonderanno in una stessa persona. Per molto tempo siamo vissuti con l'assurda persuasione che l'arte fosse un tipo di attività distinta da tutte le altre forme dell'intelligenza umana, e che le sue sole fonti e origini risiedessero nella personalità dell'artista stesso e nella sua capricciosa immaginazione"»[2] Anche se né l'insistenza di Giedion sull'«anonimità» dell'opera dell'ingegnere né il riferimento di Davioud all'«immaginazione capricciosa» dell'artista si attagliano alla forte originalità di Calatrava, quest'ultimo sembra tuttavia possedere i requisiti per rendere possibile l'accordo fra ingegneria e architettura propugnato dall'architetto francese.

L'EREDITÀ DEGLI INGEGNERI E DEGLI ARTISTI

Il catalogo dell'esposizione di Calatrava tenutasi nel 1993 al Museum of Modern Art di New York sottolinea la stretta relazione tra la sua opera e quella di altri ingegneri che hanno aperto nuove vie: «Calatrava appartiene all'importante patrimonio dell'ingegneria del XX secolo. Come i grandi esponenti della precedente generazione – Robert Maillart, Pier Luigi Nervi, Eduardo Torroja e Félix Candela – Calatrava va oltre un approccio che si limita alla soluzione di problemi tecnici. Per questi ingegneri la struttura nasce dall'equilibrio tra il criterio scientifico dell'efficienza e l'introduzione di nuove forme. Calatrava ritiene l'ingegneria "l'arte del possibile" e cerca un nuovo vocabolario formale che, pur basato sul know-how tecnico, non sia un inno alle tecniche».[3] Il primo degli ingegneri sopra citati, Robert Maillart (1872–1940), dopo essersi laureato all'ETH di Zurigo nel 1894, ha creato alcuni dei più spettacolari ponti moderni utilizzando in modo innovativo il cemento armato. Il suo magazzino per Giesshübel a Zurigo (1910) si avvale per la prima volta di un «solaio a fungo» realizzato con lastre di calcestruzzo, che consente a Maillart di ovviare al sistema della travatura. Come scrive Matilda McQuaid: «Maillart è stato uno dei primi ingegneri

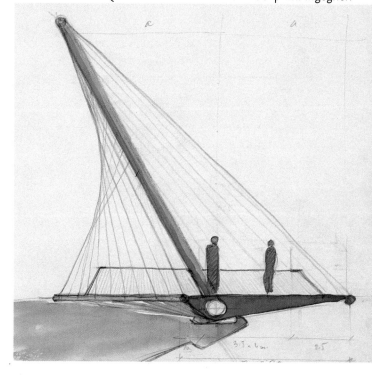

com a alvenaria e a aplicar soluções tecnicamente apropriadas e elegantes à construção em betão armado.» Se o conceito técnico não constitui a primeira motivação de Calatrava, como acontecia com Maillart, nem é, contudo, menosprezado, é inegável que alimenta a expressão global das suas estruturas. A sua obra torna-se assim um «entrelaçamento de expressão plástica e revelação estrutural, produzindo resultados que poderão ser mais bem descritos como a síntese de estética e física estrutural.»[4]

Malgrado a sua admiração natural pelo trabalho de Maillart, Santiago Calatrava apressa-se a frisar que as suas pontes são muito diferentes daquelas do seu predecessor, começando pela sua localização. «As pontes de Maillart», nota, «situam-se frequentemente no meio de uma magnífica paisagem montanhosa. O seu triunfo assenta na introdução bem sucedida de elementos artificiais em tais espaços. Creio que uma das tarefas actuais mais importantes é repensar as periferias das cidades. A maior parte das vezes, o trabalho realizado pelas colectividades nessas áreas é de teor puramente funcional; ainda que situadas perto de caminhos-de-ferro ou de cursos de água poluídos, as pontes podem exercer um efeito extraordinariamente positivo sobre o meio. Ao criar um ambiente apropriado, colocam-se em posição de oferecer um impacto simbólico cujas ramificações ultrapassam a sua localização imediata.»[5]

A obra de Calatrava é indubitavelmente influenciada pela de Félix Candela, o qual, tendo nascido em Madrid no ano de 1910, emigrara para o México em 1939, onde construiu um sem-número de estruturas notáveis em betão, como é exemplo a Iglesia de la Virgen Milagrosa (Navarte, México, 1955), edificada inteiramente à base de parabolóides hiperbólicos. Durante o mesmo período, outro espanhol, o engenheiro madrileno Eduardo Torroja (1900–1961), fica encantado pelas formas orgânicas ou vegetais, cuja presença escultural inegável poderá advir da influência de Gaudí. Como observa Matilda McQuaid, apesar de Calatrava exercer a sua profissão em Zurique, muitas das suas referências são espanholas ou, mais especificamente, ligadas a arquitectos e artistas catalães. De facto, não é por acaso que nutre uma admiração particular por pintores e escultores. «O que me fascina na personalidade de Goya, por exemplo», diz, « é que ele tenha sido um dos primeiros artistas a renunciar – como Rembrandt já o fizera – à ideia de servir um mestre. Eu admiro o silêncio da obra de Miró, bem como a sua atitude de rejeição radical perante todas as convenções.» Ainda que Gaudí lhe proporcione um exemplo, tal como Maillart, Calatrava parece mais à vontade quando fala de um artista como o escultor Julio Gonzalez. «O pai e o avô de Gonzalez eram metalúrgicos e trabalhavam para Gaudí, tendo colaborado em projectos como o Parque Güell. Depois, instalaram--se em Paris, e é aí que reside a origem do trabalho em metal de Julio Gonzalez. Com toda a modéstia», conclui o arquitecto, «podemos afirmar que o nosso trabalho é uma continuação natural da obra de Gaudí e de Gonzalez, um trabalho de artesãos evoluindo na direcção da arte abstracta.»[6]

< Campo Volantin Footbridge, Bilbao, Spain
> Trinity Bridge, Salford, England

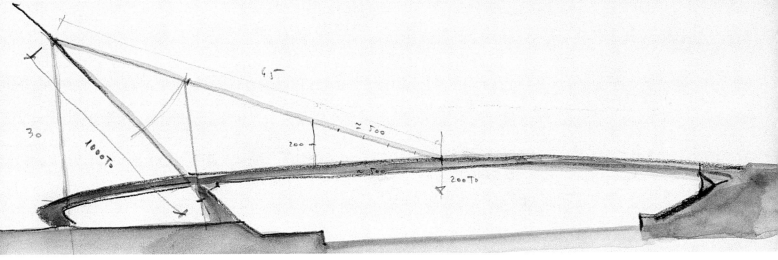

Matilda McQuaid dice al respecto: «Maillart fue uno de los primeros ingenieros de este siglo en romper con la construcción de mampostería y en aplicar soluciones elegantes y técnicamente apropiadas para la construcción en hormigón armado. A pesar de que en la obra de Calatrava el aspecto técnico no tiene carácter prioritario —como era el caso de Maillart— ni está absolutamente subordinado, marca la expresión global de lo que construye. Sus obras se convierten en un 'entrelazamiento' de la expresión plástica y la revelación estructural; el mejor modo de concebir sus construcciones es describirlas como una síntesis de estética y estructura.»[4]

Aunque naturalmente admira la obra de Maillart, a Santiago Calatrava le parece importante señalar que sus puentes son muy diferentes de los de su predecesor, aunque sólo sea por su situación. «Los puentes de Maillart —sostiene Calatrava— suelen estar ubicados en un bello escenario montañoso. Su acierto fue lograr la integración de un elemento artificial en ese magnífico entorno. Hoy en día, pienso que una de las tareas más importantes es reconsiderar la periferia de las ciudades. Muy frecuentemente, las obras públicas de esas áreas son puramente funcionales; sin embargo, incluso cerca de las vías del ferrocarril o cuando franquean ríos contaminados, los puentes pueden causar un efecto extraordinariamente positivo. Creando el entorno apropiado, pueden tener un impacto simbólico con consecuencias que van mucho más allá de la localización inmediata.»[5]

Las obras de Calatrava revelan indudables influencias de Félix Candela quien, después de nacer en Madrid en 1910, emigró a México en 1939, donde construyó una serie de interesantes estructuras de láminas de hormigón como la Iglesia de la Milagrosa de Navarte (México, 1955), un diseño basado completamente en paraboloides hiperbólicos. Otro español, el ingeniero madrileño Eduardo Torroja (1900–1961), se sintió especialmente atraído por las formas orgánicas y vegetales; su uso, con una innegable apariencia escultural, probablemente se deba a la influencia de Gaudí. Como ha señalado Matilda McQuaid, aunque Calatrava viva en Zúrich,

del nostro secolo a rompere totalmente con la costruzione in muratura e ad applicare alla struttura in cemento armato una soluzione tecnicamente appropriata ed elegante. Anche se nel lavoro di Calatrava la ricerca tecnica non è la motivazione primaria, come nel caso di Maillart, essa non va nemmeno sottostimata, perché informa l'espressione globale della struttura. Il suo lavoro diventa un "intreccio di espressione plastica e di rivelazione strutturale, producendo dei risultati che possono essere efficacemente descritti come una sintesi di estetica e fisica strutturale"»[4].

Per quanto naturalmente ammiri il lavoro di Maillart, Calatrava si affretta a far notare che i suoi ponti sono molto diversi da quelli del suo predecessore, se non altro per la loro ubicazione. «I ponti di Maillart», afferma, «sono spesso situati in magnifici paesaggi montagnosi. La sua grandezza è stata quella di saper introdurre un elemento artificiale in luoghi di tale bellezza. Credo che oggi uno dei compiti più importanti sia quello di riconsiderare la periferia delle città. Il più delle volte i grandi interventi pubblici in tali aree sono puramente funzionali, eppure, anche vicino a binari ferroviari o quando scavalcano fiumi inquinati, i ponti possono avere un effetto straordinariamente positivo. Creando un ambiente appropriato, possono avere un impatto simbolico le cui ramificazioni si estendono molto al di là della loro ubicazione immediata.»[5]

Il lavoro di Calatrava è stato senza dubbio influenzato da quello di Félix Candela che, nato a Madrid nel 1910, emigrò nel 1939 in Messico, dove realizzò una serie di edifici con leggerissime coperture in cemento armato, tra cui la Iglesia de la Virgen Milagrosa (Navarte, Messico, 1955), interamente basata sui paraboloidi iperbolici. Un altro spagnolo, l'ingegnere madrileno Eduardo Torroja (1900–1961), era affascinato dalle forme organiche o vegetali, la cui innegabile presenza scultorea non è forse estranea all'ascendente di Gaudí. Come sottolinea Matilda McQuaid, sebbene Calatrava operi a Zurigo, molti suoi riferimenti

> CH 91 Floating Concrete Pavilion, Lake Luzern, 1989

Maqueta nº ① pavellon flotante sobre el lago
Lucerna

muchas de sus referencias son españolas y particularmente catalanas, tanto de arquitectos como de artistas. No es casualidad que admire principalmente a pintores y escultores. «Lo que me atrae tanto de la personalidad de Goya, por ejemplo —declara Calatrava— es que fue uno de los primeros artistas, como Rembrandt antes que él, en renunciar a la idea de servir a cualquier maestro. Lo que admiro en la obra de Miró —añade— es su memorable silencio y su radical rechazo de todo lo convencional.» Pese a que Gaudí, y también Maillart, le hayan proporcionado modelos, Calatrava prefiere hablar de artistas como el escultor Julio González. «El padre y el abuelo de González trabajaron el metal para Gaudí en proyectos como el Parque Güell. Después se trasladaron a París; éste es el origen del trabajo de Julio González con el metal. Con la debida modestia —concluye Calatrava— se podría decir que lo que nosotros hacemos es una continuación natural de la obra de Gaudí y de González, una obra de artesanos evolucionando hacia el arte abstracto.»[6]

El arte al que se refiere Santiago Calatrava se materializa particularmente en sus puentes y construcciones de mayor éxito; sin embargo, resulta difícil expresarlo en palabras. Otra de esas figuras esenciales en la ingeniería del siglo XX, el italiano Pier Luigi Nervi, intentó hallar una definición en una serie de ponencias que dio en Harvard en 1961: «Es muy difícil explicar la razón de nuestra inmediata admiración por determinadas formas procedentes del mundo físico, con las que a primera vista nada tenemos que ver. ¿Por qué, nos satisfacen y nos conmueven esas formas de la misma manera que los objetos naturales, como las flores, las plantas y los paisajes, a los que nos hemos acostumbrado en el curso de innumerables generaciones? Hay que hacer notar que esas proezas de la naturaleza tienen en común una esencia estructural: la necesaria ausencia de cualquier decoración, una pureza de líneas y formas, más que suficientes para definir un estilo auténtico, un estilo que yo denomino estilo verdadero. Por supuesto que soy consciente de la dificultad de encontrar las palabras correctas para expresar este concepto.»

si collegano ad architetti e artisti spagnoli, e più specificamente catalani. Non è un caso che ammiri soprattutto i pittori e gli scultori. «Quello che mi affascina nella personalità di Goya, per esempio», spiega Calatrava, «è il fatto che sia stato uno dei primi artisti – sulle orme di Rembrandt – a rinunciare all'idea di servire un padrone. Quello che ammiro in Miró è il suo straordinario silenzio, oltre al suo radicale rifiuto di ogni convenzione.» Benché Gaudí, come Maillart, gli fornisca un esempio, Calatrava sembra essere più a suo agio nel parlare di un artista come lo scultore Julio Gonzalez.

«Il padre e il nonno di Gonzalez, operai metallurgici, hanno lavorato per Gaudí su progetti come il Parque Güell. Poi si sono trasferiti a Parigi, ed è lì che Gonzalez ha iniziato a creare con il metallo. Con tutta la dovuta modestia», conclude Calatrava, «si può dire che quello che noi facciamo è la naturale continuazione del lavoro di Gaudí e di Gonzalez, un lavoro di artigiani che si evolve verso l'arte astratta.»[6]

La forma d'arte cui si riferisce Calatrava è palese nei suoi ponti ed edifici più riusciti, e tuttavia è difficile descriverla a parole. Un altro dei grandi esponenti dell'ingegneria del XX secolo, l'italiano Pier Luigi Nervi, ha tentato di darne una definizione in una serie di conferenze tenute ad Harvard nel 1961: «È difficile spiegare la ragione per cui approviamo d'acchito delle forme che derivano da un mondo fisico con cui, apparentemente, non abbiamo alcun legame diretto di sorta. Perché queste forme ci soddisfano e ci toccano alla stessa stregua delle cose della natura, come i fiori, le piante, i paesaggi cui siamo abituati da innumerevoli generazioni? Si può inoltre osservare che queste realizzazioni hanno in comune un'essenza strutturale, un'assenza necessaria di ogni decorazione, una purezza di linea e di forma più che sufficienti per definire uno stile autentico, uno stile che ho chiamato "stile veritiero". Mi rendo conto di quanto sia difficile trovare le parole giuste per esprimere questo concetto».

Calatrava: «Quando parlo di queste cose con qualche amico,

A forma de arte a que se refere Calatrava é particularmente evidente nas suas pontes e edifícios mais bem sucedidos, mas continua linguisticamente impossível de descrever. Uma das outras figuras fundamentais da engenharia deste século, o italiano Pier Luigi Nervi, tenta alcançar uma definição através de uma série de conferências que deu em Harvard no ano de 1961: «É difícil explicar a razão pela qual aprovamos de modo instantâneo formas que nos chegam de um mundo físico, com o qual não mantemos, pelo menos aparentemente, qualquer tipo de ligação directa. Por que é que estas formas nos satisfazem e nos comovem da mesma maneira que o fazem os objectos da natureza, como as paisagens, as plantas e as flores, aos quais nos habituámos ao longo de inúmeras gerações? Devemos também notar que esses progressos têm em comum uma essência estrutural, uma ausência necessária de todo o ornamento, uma pureza de linhas e formas mais que suficientes para definir um estilo autêntico, o qual qualifiquei como verdadeiro. Compreendo quão difícil é encontrar as palavras exactas para expressar este conceito.»

Desenvolve Calatrava: «Quando apresento estas observações aos meus amigos, respondem-me com frequência que tal visão de um futuro próximo é terrivelmente triste, e que será talvez melhor renunciar voluntariamente a um novo estreitamento dos laços entre as nossas criações e as leis da física, se de facto isso nos conduzir a uma monotonia fatal. Não creio que esse pessimismo se justifique. Tão constrangedoras quanto possam ser as exigências técnicas, permanecerá sempre em aberto uma certa margem de liberdade para que a personalidade do criador se afirme, e, se ele for um artista, para permitir que a sua criação, mesmo dentro de uma acepção puramente técnica, se possa tornar uma obra de arte real e genuína.»

UMA DIALÉCTICA DE TRANSGRESSÃO

A permanência de Calatrava em Zurique prende-se com razões circunstanciais. Depois de ter completado os seus estudos, continuou aí ao lado de sua esposa, Robertina, de origem sueca, que não tinha ainda feito os seus. Posteriormente, sinal do destino, vence em 1982 o concurso para projectar a nova estação ferroviária de Stadelhofen (1983–1990). Este edifício invulgar encontra-se bem localizado: situado numa colina verdejante perto de Bellevue-Platz e da Theater-Strasse, junto ao lago, está perfeitamente integrado num ambiente urbano de cariz tradicional. «Para compreender esta estação», explica Calatrava, «é necessário observá-la como um projecto extremamente urbano, uma daquelas intervenções que contribuem para o restauro do tecido urbano. Representa um contraste muito vincado entre o radicalismo das opções técnicas e arquitectónicas e a atitude em relação à cidade, a qual é de extrema suavidade. Foram criados múltiplos vínculos – em relação não só às pontes e aos acessos, mas também às correspondências entre as ruas, que não existiam. Conceberam-se também inúmeros pequenos espaços verdes, como o manto de verdura suspenso

< Stadelhofen Railway Station, Zurich, Switzerland
> Stadelhofen Railway Station, Zurich, Switzerland

Acerca de esto, Calatrava sostiene: «Cuando hablo de estos asuntos con mis amigos, me suelen decir que esa visión de futuro próximo es terriblemente triste, que quizá sería mejor renunciar voluntariamente a estrechar más los lazos entre nuestras creaciones y las leyes de la física, si al parecer éstas nos conducen a una fatal monotonía. Yo no veo justificación para este pesimismo. Por mucho que los requerimientos técnicos nos constriñan, siempre queda suficiente margen de libertad para ver la personalidad del que ha creado esa obra y para permitir que su obra, si realmente se trata de un artista, se convierta —incluso cuando obedece estrictamente a las exigencias técnicas— en una verdadera obra de arte.»[7]

LA DIALECTICA DE LA TRANSGRESION

El hecho de que Calatrava resida en Zúrich desde hace veinte años se debe a las circunstancias: cuando terminó sus estudios permaneció en Suiza para que su esposa Robertina, de origen sueco, pudiera acabar los suyos. La suerte quiso que en 1982 ganara el concurso abierto para la nueva Estación de Ferrocarril de Stadelhofen (1983–1990). Esta extraordinaria construcción se encuentra en un lugar absolutamente céntrico. La estación linda con una colina de zonas verdes cerca de la Bellevue Platz y de la Theaterstrasse y se encuentra perfectamente integrada en un entorno urbano en su mayor parte tradicional. «Para entender la Estación de Ferrocarril de Stadelhofen —expone Calatrava— hay que considerarla como un proyecto eminentemente urbano que impone una restauración de la trama urbana. Marca un claro contraste entre el radicalismo de la solución técnica y arquitectónica que se ha seleccionado y la actitud frente a la ciudad, extraordinariamente comedida. Se crearon numerosos enlaces —no sólo puentes y puntos de acceso, sino también conexiones con las calles de alrededor, que anteriormente no existían—. Y también se emplazaron pequeños espacios verdes como una cubierta de césped por encima del nivel superior.» Cuando el visitante se aproxima a la estación desde el centro de la ciudad, se encuentra en primer lugar el edificio tradicional, en el que

spesso mi sento dire che questa visione del futuro prossimo è deprimente, che forse sarebbe meglio rinunciare volontariamente a stringere ancor più i legami tra le nostre creazioni e le leggi fisiche, se davvero questi legami devono indurci a una fatale monotonia. Non trovo giustificato questo pessimismo. Per quanto le esigenze tecniche possano essere vincolanti, rimane sempre un margine di libertà sufficiente perché la personalità del creatore di un'opera si possa esprimere e, se si tratta di un artista, per consentire che la sua creazione, pur nella stretta obbedienza alla tecnica, diventi una vera e autentica opera d'arte».[7]

UNA DIALETTICA DI TRASGRESSIONE

La permanenza di Calatrava a Zurigo è frutto delle circostanze. Terminati gli studi, si è trattenuto nella città svizzera perché la moglie Robertina, di origini svedesi, non aveva ancora completato i suoi. Poi, per un caso del destino, nel 1982 Calatrava vince un concorso per il progetto della nuova stazione ferroviaria di Stadelhofen (1983–90). Sarebbe un eufemismo dire che questo singolare edificio si trova in una posizione centrale. Incastonato sul fianco di una collina verdeggiante vicino a Bellevue-Platz e non lontano da Theater-Strasse e dal lago, è strettamente integrato in un ambiente urbano in prevalenza tradizionale. «Per capire la stazione ferroviaria di Stadelhofen», afferma l'architetto-ingegnere «occorre vederla come un progetto squisitamente urbano, un progetto che ha comportato la ridefinizione del tessuto urbano. C'è un netto contrasto tra la natura radicale delle soluzioni tecniche e architettoniche adottate e l'atteggiamento verso la città, che è estremamente rispettoso. È stata creata una molteplicità di collegamenti: non soltanto ponti e punti di accesso, ma anche connessioni con le vie circostanti che prima non esistevano. Si sono ricavati dei piccoli spazi verdi, come quello situato sopra il livello superiore.» Il visitatore che si avvicina alla stazione provenendo dalla città si vede davanti un padiglione molto tradizionale (la sede originale della stazione) prima di entrare

sobre o nível superior.» Com efeito, quando se aproxima da estação vindo da cidade, o visitante encontra primeiro o pavilhão tradicional, que albergava a estação, antes de descer ou penetrar nas áreas projectadas por Calatrava. «Tornou-se evidente desde o início», continua o arquitecto, «que o respeito devotado na Suíça às construções com mais de cem anos eliminaria toda a tentativa de demolir ou modificar substancialmente as antigas instalações. Não considerei essa ideia ilógica, pois correspondia a uma certa interpretação da cidade que tinha permanecido intacta.»[8] Uma vez transposto o velho pavilhão, o visitante descobre um mundo assaz diferente, que se aproxima mais do imaginário de Gaudí do que daquele dos impávidos arquitectos de Zurique. Apesar de Calatrava salientar que Zurique possui uma espécie de tradição arquitectónica radical, patente nas casas de arquitectos como Marcel Breuer, é certo que esta estação lhe concedeu a primeira grande ocasião de pôr em prática um tipo de concepção inovadora que acabaria por lhe trazer a notoriedade.

Os trabalhos de construção desenrolaram-se, nesse local em ângulo curvo de 40 por 270 m, sem interferir com o tráfego dos comboios. A certa altura, a operação sofreu alterações através da inclusão de uma zona comercial subterrânea. O conjunto apresenta uma unidade orgânica, malgrado os constrangimentos que não simplificaram os trabalhos. Qual extravagante dinossauro voador aninhado na encosta da colina, a estrutura articula-se através de elementos repetitivos, interrompidos por enormes portas antropomórficas que conduzem até ao centro comercial subterrâneo, onde depressa se fica com a impressão de se estar no ventre do monstro. Existe uma continuidade entre o metal escuro utilizado acima do solo e a armação tipo costelas em betão abaixo que determina uma clara hierarquia de espaços e formas, realçando a legibilidade e a claridade funcional da estação.

Embora o conjunto que compõe a estação de Stadelhofen sugira uma metáfora de um animal pré--histórico, a substância dos planos de Calatrava é mais complexa, ou talvez diferente. «Na realidade, enveredei por aquilo que poderei denominar como uma dialéctica de transgressão, a qual está alicerçada no vocabulário das forças estruturais. Em Stadelhofen, por exemplo, encontra-se uma série de colunas inclinadas. Ainda que a sua construção pareça evidenciar uma opção estética, foi de facto determinada pela necessidade de sustentar a estrutura. Naturalmente, dispunha de muitas outras soluções para o problema. Poderia ter desenhado simples cilindros, por exemplo, mas optei por uma articulação em forma de mão. É aqui que o problema da metáfora se torna interessante. Como poderia ter expressado melhor a função das colunas se não lhes tivesse atribuído o sentido do gesto físico de transportar?»[9]

O nome de Santiago Calatrava é bastante citado quando se fala de pontes, mas é também sinónimo de um especialista de renome em estações ferroviárias. Encontra-se agora debruçado, por exemplo, sobre novos projectos em Lisboa e Liège. A estação de TGV de Lyon-Satolas (1989–1994) foi uma das realizações que mais contribuiu para o seu prestígio. Esta construção de 5600 m^2, localizada

> Stadelhofen Railway Station, Zurich, Switzerland

se hallaba la antigua estación, antes de entrar o descender a las áreas diseñadas por Calatrava. «Resultaba obvio —continúa exponiendo el propio arquitecto— que el respeto que se tiene en Suiza por cualquier edificio de más de cien años de antigüedad eliminaba cualquier posibilidad de derribar o de modificar sustancialmente la estación. Me parece lógico, sin embargo, porque responde a la idea de la ciudad como unidad intacta.»[8] Pero, antes de que el viajero salga del antiguo pabellón, entra en un mundo diferente que parece mucho más relacionado con la imaginación de Gaudí que con los impasibles ciudadanos zuriqueses. Aunque Calatrava subraya que Zúrich tiene una cierta tradición de arquitectura moderna, con casas construidas por arquitectos como Marcel Breuer, está claro que la Estación de Ferrocarril de Stadelhofen fue el primer proyecto a gran escala que consiguió llevar a cabo con ese tipo de diseño innovador que le ha hecho famoso.

Sobre este terreno en forma de arco, en una superficie de 40 x 270 metros, se construyó la nueva estación sin interrumpir el tráfico de trenes de cercanías; a un nivel subterráneo se incluyó un centro comercial. El conjunto se caracteriza por su unidad orgánica; en esas circunstancias no podría ser más sencillo. Como un extravagante dinosaurio volador que ha venido a anidar a un flanco de la colina, se articula con elementos que se repiten, con enormes puertas antropomorfas que conducen al centro comercial subterráneo, donde el visitante pronto tiene la impresión de encontrarse en el vientre de hormigón del monstruo. La continuidad de los perfiles metálicos de color oscuro a nivel del terreno y los pilares de hormigón en forma de costillas en el subsuelo establecen una jerarquía inequívoca de espacios y formas, mientras que el énfasis se pone en la lectura y la claridad funcional de la estación.

Si bien la estación de Stadelhofen puede dar la impresión de haber sido concebida siguiendo una especie de metáfora de dinosaurio, la sustancia del diseño de Calatrava es más compleja, o quizá sencillamente diferente. «En realidad, lo que estaba buscando es lo que yo denomino 'dialéctica de la transgresión', que se basa en

o scendere nelle aree specificamente concepite da Calatrava. «Era ovvio fin dall'inizio», continua l'architetto, «che il rispetto testimoniato in Svizzera per gli edifici di oltre cent'anni precludeva ogni tentativo di demolire o di modificare radicalmente la vecchia struttura della stazione. È un punto di vista che tuttavia non trovo illogico, perché si accorda con una lettura della città che rimane intatta.»[8] Una volta oltrepassato il padiglione, però, il visitatore entra in un mondo molto diverso, più in sintonia con l'immaginazione di Gaudí che con quella dei flemmatici abitanti di Zurigo. Sebbene Calatrava segnali che Zurigo possiede una certa tradizione di architettura radicale, con case firmate da architetti come Marcel Breuer, è evidente che la stazione di Stadelhofen gli ha offerto la prima opportunità della sua carriera di dare espressione su vasta scala al tipo di concezione innovativa che lo avrebbe reso famoso.

La costruzione della nuova stazione, che sorge su un sito curviforme di 40 x 270 m, ha dovuto essere effettuata senza ostacolare il traffico dei treni pendolari. La struttura include anche un centro commerciale sotterraneo e l'insieme ha una sua unità organica, malgrado le circostanze non siano state esattamente favorevoli. Come un bizzarro dinosauro volante che è venuto a rannicchiarsi sul fianco della collina, la stazione si articola in una serie di elementi ripetitivi, con enormi porte antropomorfiche che conducono al centro commerciale sotterraneo, dove si ha la netta impressione di trovarsi proprio nella pancia dell'animale. C'è una continuità tra il metallo scuro utilizzato in superficie e le nervature in cemento dell'area sottostante che stabiliscono una chiara gerarchia di spazi e forme, dando al tempo stesso un ovvio rilievo alla leggibilità e alla chiarezza funzionale della stazione. Tuttavia, per quanto il complesso della stazione ferroviaria di Stadelhofen possa dare l'impressione di essere stato concepito attorno alla metafora di un dinosauro, la sostanza del progetto di Calatrava è più complessa, o forse diversa. «In realtà, quello che ho tentato di fare lo definirei una dialettica della trasgressione,

sobre o aeroporto de Satolas, pertence àquela nova geração de edifícios concebidos para acompanhar o desenvolvimento da rede francesa de comboios de alta velocidade (TGV). A justaposição dos transportes ferroviários, aéreos e locais num único local compõe um sistema particularmente eficaz. Com 120 m de comprimento, 100 de largura e 40 de altura, a estação de passageiros, inaugurada em 7 de Julho de 1994, está apoiada sobre um elemento central em aço que pesa 1300 toneladas. Sugerindo um pássaro em voo, assemelha-se ao terminal construído por Eero Saarinen no Aeroporto Kennedy (E.V.A.) (1957–1962), embora seja mais exuberante que o seu antecessor americano. O plano desse complexo, com a ligação ao aeroporto, lembra igualmente uma raia. Um total de seis linhas ferroviárias estendem-se sob o edifício principal e os comboios detêm-se ante uma plataforma coberta com 500 m de comprimento, também desenhada pelo arquitecto. As linhas centrais, concebidas para os comboios que atravessam a estação a mais de 300 km/h, estão encerradas numa couraça de betão, um sistema que exigiu cálculos cuidadosos sobre as «ondas de choque» que rodeiam o TGV. Financiado pela companhia nacional de caminhos-de-ferro francesa (SNCF), pela região de Rhône-Alpes e pelo Departamento de Rhône, o custo total deste equipamento ultrapassou os 600 milhões de francos.

Quando confrontado com a tal imagem do pássaro pré-histórico, Calatrava responde de uma forma tipicamente evasiva, ainda que plena de elementos informativos: «Eu sou essencialmente um arquitecto», afirma, «e não um artista ou alguém que procura fomentar uma revolução. É interessante notar que, no seu romance *Notre-Dame de Paris*, Victor Hugo compara a catedral a um monstro pré-histórico. Mesmo que tivesse excelentes conhecimentos de arquitectura e que tenha sido um escritor muito consciencioso, o facto é que não se coibiu de recorrer a uma metáfora tão inesperada para descrever Notre-Dame. Francamente, não estou à procura de metáforas. Nunca imaginei um pássaro; antes, foquei-me numa pesquisa que qualifico por vezes sem modéstia como escultura.»[10] De facto, os desenhos e as esculturas de Calatrava, que se aproximam mais de Satolas, parecem ter encontrado a sua origem não na metáfora de um pássaro, mas no estudo do olho e da pálpebra, um mote recorrente na sua obra. «O olho», refere, «é a verdadeira ferramenta do arquitecto, e esta ideia remonta aos babilónios.»

A frente arqueada da estação de Satolas, a qual mergulha a direito no solo, tem sido comparada ao bico de um pássaro, mas Calatrava, uma vez mais, parece ter em mente uma ideia completamente diferente. «O "bico" é o resultado de um cálculo complexo sobre as forças que jogam na estrutura. É também o ponto de confluência das condutas de escoamento das águas. Naturalmente, esforcei-me por minimizar a massa nesse ponto, mas sem qualquer intenção antropomórfica», explica. Admitindo que o uso que faz das suas próprias esculturas como ponto de partida para os seus projectos possa ser considerado mais como um escolha estética do que um conceito

> Lyon-Satolas Airport Railway Station, Lyon, France

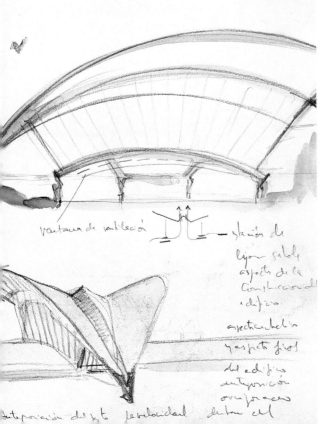

el lenguaje formal de las fuerzas estructurales. En Stadelhofen, por ejemplo, hay una serie de pilares inclinados. Aunque parezca una solución estética, se deben realmente a una necesidad estructural. Naturalmente había diversas soluciones para este tipo de soporte; por ejemplo, habría podido diseñar simples cilindros, pero preferí articularlos como los dedos de una mano. Aquí es donde la cuestión de la metáfora gana interés: ¿qué mejor modo de expresar esta función de los pilares que colocándolos de un modo que recuerden el gesto físico de sostener?»[9]

A pesar de que el nombre de Santiago Calatrava se suele asociar a puentes, también es un reconocido especialista en la construcción de estaciones de ferrocarril; por ejemplo, actualmente está trabajando en grandes proyectos para las estaciones de Lisboa y de Lieja. Uno de los edificios que más ha contribuido a esta reputación fue la Terminal del TGV en Lyón-Satolas (1989–1994). Esta estación de ferrocarril, de 5.600 metros cuadrados, situada en el Aeropuerto de Satolas, es una de las instalaciones de nueva generación, construidas en Francia para la creciente red de trenes de alta velocidad (TGV). La conjunción en un mismo lugar del ferrocarril, el avión y los medios de transporte locales crea un sistema de particular eficacia. Con sus 120 metros de longitud, 100 de anchura y 40 de altura, esta terminal de pasajeros —inaugurada el 7 de julio de 1994— se basa en un elemento central de acero de 1300 toneladas. Al sugerir la forma de un pájaro en pleno vuelo, la estación de Calatrava parece hacerse eco de la TWA Terminal en el Kennedy Airport (1957–1962), obra de Eero Saarinen; pero sus formas son incluso más exuberantes que las de su predecesor norteamericano. La planta del complejo, incluyendo la conexión con el aeropuerto, recuerda también la forma de una manta raya. Por debajo del edificio principal se encuentran seis vías por las que transitan los trenes, que paran en andenes cubiertos de 500 metros de longitud, igualmente diseñados por el arquitecto. Las vías centrales, pensadas para trenes de alta velocidad, que circulan a más de 300 kilómetros por hora, están cubiertas por una retícula de hormigón, un sistema que requiere un cálculo

basata sul vocabolario delle forze strutturali. A Stadelhofen, per esempio, c'è una serie di colonne inclinate. Anche se questa ha tutta l'aria di essere una scelta estetica, in realtà è stata determinata dalla necessità di sostenere la struttura. Naturalmente erano possibili varie soluzioni per questo tipo di supporto, dei semplici cilindri per esempio, ma ho scelto un'articolazione che riprende la forma della mano. È qui che il discorso delle metafore si fa interessante. Come esprimere meglio la funzione delle colonne se non investendole del senso del gesto fisico di sorreggere?»[9]

Anche se il suo nome viene spesso citato in rapporto alla costruzione di ponti, Calatrava è anche uno specialista riconosciuto in stazioni ferroviarie. Attualmente è per esempio impegnato nella realizzazione di vaste installazioni di questo tipo a Lisbona e a Liegi. Uno dei lavori che ha maggiormente contribuito alla sua fama è tuttavia il terminal dei TGV di Lione-Satolas (1989–94). Questa stazione che occupa un'area di 5600 m² è situata all'aeroporto di Satolas ed è parte di una nuova generazione di strutture concepite per servire la rete sempre più vasta di treni ad alta velocità (TGV) in Francia. La concentrazione in un unico sito di servizi di trasporto ferroviario, aereo e locale è un sistema particolarmente efficace. Lungo 120 m, largo 100 e alto 40, il terminal passeggeri, inaugurato il 7 luglio 1994, si basa su un elemento centrale in acciaio del peso di 1300 tonnellate. Con la sua silhouette che ricorda un uccello in volo, la stazione di Calatrava sembra richiamare il terminal della TWA realizzato da Eero Saarinen al Kennedy Airport (1957–62), ma è più esuberante del progetto americano. La planimetria del complesso, con la passerella che lo collega al terminal dell'aeroporto, fa pensare a una manta. Sotto l'edificio principale corrono sei linee ferroviarie e i treni si fermano lungo marciapiedi coperti per un tratto di 500 m, anch'essi disegnati da Calatrava. I binari centrali, destinati ai treni in transito che viaggiano a una velocità di oltre 300 chilometri orari, sono racchiusi in un guscio

antropomórfico, Calatrava acrescenta: «Podem considerar irracional, mas diria que não existem pistas a seguir. Desejo ser como um navio no mar: atrás, a esteira, e nada pela frente».[11]

Um projecto mais recente de Calatrava para a estação de TGV em Liège testemunha a evolução do seu pensamento, ilustrando certas razões para a diferença entre a forma apurada das suas pontes e a impressão mais complexa e aparentemente «antropomórfica» dos seus edifícios maiores. «Pela sua própria natureza, as pontes exigem uma economia de meios rigorosa. Cada parte – tabuleiro, arcos de suporte e alicerces – representa cerca de um terço do custo. Dada a simplicidade funcional de uma ponte, a margem de intervenção é muito limitada. Por outro lado, numa estação ferroviária existem pelo menos seis tipos de decisões que podem provocar, cada uma por si, um impacto estético, desde a escolha dos caixilhos metálicos das janelas até ao plano de iluminação. Cabe ao talento do criador encontrar a solução por ele imaginada dentro das restrições económicas de tal projecto.» Apesar desta problemática essencialmente distinta, pode ser confirmada de imediato que a inclinação de Calatrava para a «transgressão», ou inovação, o atrai para a concepção de pontes invulgares e estações surpreendentes. «Tomemos o exemplo da nova estação de TGV em Liège», continua. «Reinventámos completamente a fachada. Ou melhor, deixou de existir a fachada tradicional, o que é, a meu ver, uma transgressão fundamental. Em vez dela, haverá apenas grandes aberturas, denunciadas por telheiros de metal suspensos sobre a praça em frente à estação.» Contudo, como nota Calatrava, esta opção tem importantes consequências ao nível da composição funcional do local. Como é que uma estação sem fachada poderá ser identificada enquanto tal? «O cenário é urbano, e pareceu-me que a primeira imagem que os passageiros ou visitantes terão da estação será a mais importante», explica o arquitecto. «A minha solução tem uma face dupla. Como o edifício está localizado sobre uma colina e é acessível de cima, oferece-nos uma vista geral sobre a cidade e sobre o conjunto da estação. O plano torna-se assim a verdadeira fachada. De modo a melhorar a relação entre a cidade e a estação, propusemos a criação de uma praça em frente desta última.»[12] Podemos pensar que esta estratégia de ausência, ou de uma espécie de minimalismo, aproxima mais o conceito desta estação daquele das pontes que de alguns dos primeiros edifícios de Calatrava. Quanto à sua tendência para a «transgressão», torna-se claro que os métodos meticulosos do arquitecto implicam o respeito pelas condições económicas e funcionais do projecto, e procuram uma dialéctica específica dentro da gama das possibilidades técnicas existentes. Não se trata de um artista em pleno devaneio, esquadrinhando esqueletos de dinossauros para forjar um qualquer conceito drástico. Como se questionou Nervi, «Por que é que estas formas nos satisfazem e nos comovem da mesma maneira que o fazem os objectos da natureza, como as paisagens, as plantas e as flores, aos quais nos habituámos ao longo de inúmeras gerações?» Sem dúvida porque brotam da imaginação fértil do arquitecto/engenheiro, mas também porque respeitam, desde o início, as principais forças em jogo.

< Lyon-Satolas Airport Railway Station, Lyon, France
> The Bird

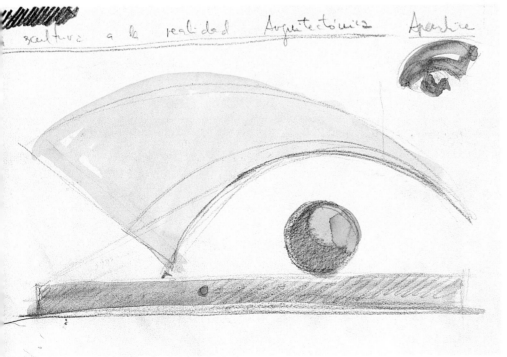

cuidadoso de la onda expansiva que desplaza el TGV. Los costes totales de este proyecto superaron los 600 millones de francos, y se repartieron entre la Compañía Nacional de los Ferrocarriles Franceses (SNCF), la región de Ródano-Alpes y el Departamento del Ródano.

Cuando se le pregunta por la imagen del ave prehistórica, Calatrava responde de ese modo indirecto y, sin embargo, tan informativo, típicamente suyo: «Yo sólo soy un mero arquitecto, no soy ni un artista ni nadie que desee desencadenar una revolución. Resulta extremadamente interesante que Víctor Hugo, en Notre-Dame de París, compare la catedral con un monstruo prehistórico. El hecho de que posiblemente fuera un excelente conocedor de la arquitectura, además de un escrupuloso escritor, no le impidió emplear esa insólita metáfora para describir la Catedral de Notre-Dame. Honradamente: yo no busco metáforas, ni tampoco pensé, en un pájaro, sino en los estudios previos que a veces pretenciosamente llamo esculturas.»[10] De hecho, tanto los dibujos de Calatrava como sus obras plásticas estrechamente relacionas con el proyecto de Satolas no parecen tener su origen en la metáfora del pájaro, sino en el estudio del ojo y del párpado, un tema recurrente en su obra. «El ojo -sostiene Calatrava- es la verdadera herramienta del arquitecto, y ésta es una idea que se remonta a los babilonios.» El pórtico en forma de doble concha de la Estación de Satolas, que parece introducirse en la tierra, ha sido comparado con el pico de un ave; pero aquí Calatrava también parece haber tenido en mente una idea completamente distinta. «El 'pico' fue el resultado de los complicados cálculos de las fuerzas que se ejercen sobre esta construcción, al mismo tiempo que es el punto de confluencia de los conductos de evacuación del agua de lluvia. Por supuesto que me esforcé, en reducir la masa de dicho punto al mínimo posible, pero en ningún momento pensé, en un diseño antropomorfo», dice. Sin embargo, admite que la utilización de sus propias esculturas como punto de partida para su proyecto puede considerarse como una cuestión meramente estética, tanto como lo hubiera sido un modelo

di cemento armato, la cui costruzione ha richiesto un calcolo estremamente accurato delle «onde d'urto» provocate dal TGV. Il progetto, dal costo totale di 600 milioni di franchi, è stato finanziato dalle ferrovie francesi (SNCF), dalla Région Rhône-Alpes e dal Départment du Rhône.

Interrogato riguardo all'immagine di un uccello preistorico, Calatrava risponde in modo tipicamente indiretto e tuttavia fornendo interessanti informazioni: «Sono soltanto un architetto e non un artista o qualcuno che tenti di fomentare una rivoluzione. Potrebbe essere interessante ricordare che, nel romanzo *Notre-Dame de Paris*, Victor Hugo paragona la cattedrale a un mostro preistorico. Malgrado potesse avere un'eccellente conoscenza dell'architettura e fosse uno scrittore molto coscienzioso, la metafora da lui usata per descrivere la cattedrale di Notre-Dame è un po' inaspettata. Onestamente, non vado in cerca di metafore. Non ho mai pensato a un uccello. La mia è piuttosto una ricerca in direzione di quella che talvolta sono abbastanza presuntuoso da chiamare scultura».[10] Infatti, sia i disegni che la scultura di Calatrava più strettamente associati a Satolas sembrano trovare la loro origine non tanto nella metafora di un uccello quanto nello studio dell'occhio e della palpebra, un tema ricorrente nelle sue opere. «L'occhio», dichiara Calatrava, «è il vero attrezzo dell'architetto, e questa è un'idea che risale ai babilonesi.» L'elemento ricurvo della stazione di Satolas, che si tuffa a capofitto nella terra, è stato paragonato al becco di un uccello, ma di nuovo Calatrava pare aver avuto in mente un'idea tutta diversa. «Il "becco"», racconta, «è il risultato di complessi calcoli delle forze che agiscono sulla struttura. Succede che sia anche il punto di confluenza delle tubature per lo scarico dell'acqua. Naturalmente ho fatto del mio meglio per ridurre al minimo la massa in quel punto, ma senza alcuna intenzione di creare un design antropomorfico.» Ammettendo che l'uso delle sue sculture come punto di partenza per il design possa rappresentare una scelta estetica alla stessa stregua di un concetto consciamente antropomorfico, Calatrava

> Lyon-Satolas Airport Railway Station, Lyon, France

consientemente antropomorfo. Y añade: «Se le puede llamar irracional si se quiere, pero pienso que éste no es el sendero a seguir. A mí me gusta ser como un barco en el mar, que va dejando una estela... pero la popa nada sabe de caminos.»[11]

Un proyecto más reciente de Calatrava, para la Estación del TGV en Lieja, muestra cierta evolución en su pensamiento e ilustra las diferencias entre la extrema sencillez de sus puentes y el carácter más complejo —y al parecer «antropomorfo»— de sus construcciones de mayores dimensiones. «Por su propia naturaleza, los puentes exigen una estricta economía de medios. Cada una de sus partes —el tablero, el arco que lo soporta y los cimientos— representa aproximadamente un tercio de los costes. Teniendo en cuenta la sencilla función de un puente, apenas queda margen de intervención. Por el contrario, en una estación hay al menos dieciséis tipos de decisiones con las que se puede producir un impacto estético: desde la selección de la carpintería metálica de las ventanas hasta la iluminación. Del talento del arquitecto depende que, con los fondos limitados de un proyecto de esas características, se consiga el resultado que ha imaginado.» Al margen de que se trate de situaciones fundamentalmente diferentes, se puede apreciar la predilección que siente Calatrava por la «transgresión» o la innovación que le lleva tanto a diseñar puentes inusuales como estaciones sorprendentes. «Por ejemplo, en la nueva Estación del TGV en Lieja —continúa—, hemos reinventado la fachada completa. O, mejor dicho, no hay fachada. Esto es lo que yo considero una transgresión radical. En lugar de una fachada tradicional sólo habrá ventanales amplios, rematados por marquesinas metálicas que sobresalen sobre la plaza a la que da la estación.» Como Calatrava subraya, esta decisión de diseño tiene consecuencias de peso para la estructura funcional de la estación. Desde un punto de vista más simbólico se puede preguntar cómo será posible identificar una estación sin fachada. «La localización es urbana y me parece que lo importante será la primera impresión que la estación cause a los visitantes o viajeros», explica Calatrava. «Presento una solución

afferma: «Può sembrare irrazionale, ma secondo me non c'è nessun percorso da seguire. Voglio essere come una barca nel mare. Dietro c'è una scia, ma davanti non si vedono rotte».[11]

Un suo progetto più recente per la stazione dei treni ad alta velocità di Liegi mostra alcuni cambiamenti nel suo modo di pensare e illustra le ragioni delle differenze tra la nuda essenzialità dei suoi ponti e l'impressione più complessa e apparentemente «antropomorfica» suscitata dai suoi edifici più grandi. «Per la loro stessa natura i ponti esigono una stretta economia di mezzi. Gli elementi di un ponte – l'impalcato, l'arco di sostegno e le fondazioni – rappresentano ciascuno circa un terzo del costo totale. Data la semplicità della funzione di un ponte, il margine d'intervento è limitato. In una stazione ferroviaria, invece, ci sono almeno sedici tipi di decisioni che possono esercitare un impatto estetico, dalla scelta degli infissi metallici delle aperture al design degli impianti di illuminazione ecc. Sta nell'abilità del progettista pervenire alle soluzioni che si era immaginato nell'ambito delle restrizioni economiche imposte dal progetto.» Nonostante questa fondamentale diversità di condizioni, è evidente che il gusto di Calatrava per la «trasgressione» o l'innovazione lo induce a progettare tanto ponti fuori del comune quanto stazioni insolite. «Prenda il caso della nuova stazione del TGV di Liegi», prosegue l'architetto ingegnere. «Abbiamo completamente reinventato la facciata. O, meglio, non c'è facciata. Una trasgressione, secondo me, fondamentale. Al posto di una facciata tradizionale ci saranno soltanto delle grandi aperture segnalate da pensiline metalliche sporgenti sul piazzale prospiciente la stazione.» Lo stesso Calatrava fa notare che questa scelta comporta notevoli conseguenze sulla disposizione funzionale dell'area. Da un punto di vista più simbolico ci si può chiedere come possa essere riconoscibile una stazione senza facciata. «Il contesto è urbano, e mi è sembrato che fosse importante la prima visione che i viaggiatori o visitatori avrebbero avuto della stazione», spiega Calatrava. «La mia soluzione è stata duplice. Poiché ci si avvicina

REDESCOBRIR A PONTE

Como afirma o próprio Santiago Calatrava, conceber uma ponte envolve uma série de problemas específicos, de que os mais simbólicos não são os menos importantes. «Se olharmos para a história das pontes nos séculos XIX e XX», refere, «muitas constituem estruturas deveras particulares, carregadas de significado. «Revestimo-las de pedra, de parapeitos ou leões esculpidos, e mesmo de anjos sustentando os lampadários, como é o caso da ponte Alexandre III, em Paris. Esta atitude desapareceu após a Segunda Guerra Mundial. Urgia então reconstruir rapidamente centenas de pontes por toda a Europa, e foi desta necessidade que nasceu a escola da ponte puramente funcional. Uma boa ponte seria aquela mais simples, e sobretudo a mais barata.» Obviamente, Calatrava pensa que esta escola funcionalista perdeu a utilidade que a tinha justificado depois da guerra. «Hoje, temos de redescobrir o potencial das pontes», declara, e cita exemplos de cidades europeias como Florença, Veneza ou Paris para sublinhar que, através da sua função e também da sua permanência, as obras de arte do passado desempenharam um papel importante na formação da imagem dessas cidades. Para resumir o seu pensamento, Calatrava chega ao ponto de afirmar que a construção de uma ponte pode-se revelar um gesto cultural ainda mais rico do que o de um novo museu. «A ponte é mais eficaz, pois está ao alcance de todos. Mesmo um iletrado pode apreciar uma ponte. Um único gesto transforma a natureza, ordenando-a. É o maior grau de eficiência que se pode atingir», conclui. [13]

O sucesso dos esforços de Calatrava no sentido de conferir um novo sentido às estruturas de travessia pode ser ilustrado pelo exemplo da ponte do Alamillo e pelo viaduto de La Cartuja (Sevilha, 1987–1992). Destacando-se numa das entradas da Expo '92, o pilão com 142 m de altura inclina-se num ângulo de 58° (idêntico as da grande pirâmide de Keops, perto do Cairo) e é visível da maior parte do centro antigo da cidade. A ponte, com uma abertura total de 200 m, atravessa o Meandro San Jeronimo, um afluente activo do rio Guadalquivir. Está suportada por 13 pares de cabos, mas, acima de tudo, o «peso do pilão repleto de betão é suficiente para contrabalançar o tabuleiro, eliminando a necessidade de cabos traseiros».[14] Calatrava concebera originalmente uma segunda ponte, inclinada na direcção oposta, como um reflexo da primeira, para atravessar o Guadalquivir, mas o orçamento obrigou o mestre de obras, a Junta da Andaluzia, a limitar-se a uma só construção, em conjunto com o viaduto da Puente de la Cartuja, com 500 m de comprimento.

Para além dos seus cadernos de notas profusamente ilustrados, os quais retratam as reflexões envolvidas na concepção primitiva do pilão do Alamillo, Calatrava inspirou-se directamente no «Torso corredor», uma escultura que criou em 1986, «na qual cubos de mármore inclinados e empilhados equilibram-se num fio metálico retesado».[15] Com efeito, muitos dos desenhos de Calatrava espalhados pelas paredes da sua casa em Zurique reproduzem figuras em movimento. Como sugere

> Station, Liège, Belgium

doble. Como se encuentra en una colina y al edificio se llega desde la parte superior, a la persona que se acerca se le ofrece una vista de la ciudad y de la disposición de la estación, que se convierte así en fachada. Para mejorar la relación entre la ciudad y la estación, proponemos crear una plaza delante de ésta.»[12] Parece que esta estrategia de la ausencia o de una especie de minimalismo hace que la Estación de Lieja tenga con los puentes de Calatrava una relación más estrecha que cualquier otra obra construida anteriormente por él. Al igual que su inclinación a las «transgresiones», los métodos de Santiago Calatrava también implican un respeto por las condiciones económicas y funcionales de un proyecto y la búsqueda de una reflexión específica en la gama de posibilidades técnicas factibles. No es un artista desfogado que remueva esqueletos de dinosaurios para encontrar una idea utilizable. A la pregunta de Nervi: «¿Por qué, nos satisfacen y nos conmueven esas formas de la misma manera que los objetos naturales, como las flores, las plantas y los paisajes, a los que nos hemos acostumbrado en el curso de innumerables generaciones?», la respuesta ha de ser: indudablemente porque surgen de la fértil imaginación del arquitecto/ingeniero, pero también porque respetan, desde un principio, las fuerzas elementales en juego.

REDESCUBRIR EL PUENTE

Como el mismo Santiago Calatrava expone, al diseñar un puente entran en juego factores muy específicos; entre ellos, los simbólicos no son los menos importantes. «Si se observa la historia de los puentes durante los siglos XIX y XX —declara Calatrava— se verá que muchos tienen una estructura muy particular, cargada de significado. Unos estaban recubiertos de piedra, otros tuvieron esculturas en forma de león o barandillas; en el puente de Alejandro III de París, incluso hay lámparas sostenidas por ángeles. Esta actitud desapareció al finalizar la Segunda Guerra Mundial. Fue necesario reconstruir con rapidez cientos de puentes en toda Europa. Por pura necesidad surgió una escuela de diseño funcional. Un buen puente era un

dall'alto all'edificio, che a sua volta è situato su una collina, si ha una veduta della città e della stazione nel suo complesso. La pianta diventa dunque la vera facciata. Per migliorare il rapporto tra la città e la stazione abbiamo proposto di creare un piazzale davanti all'edificio.»[12] Si direbbe che grazie a questa strategia dell'assenza o, in un certo senso, minimalista, la stazione di Liegi risulterà, quanto a concezione, più affine ai ponti di altri precedenti progetti di Calatrava. Per quanto riguarda il suo gusto per la «trasgressione», diventa sempre più evidente che i metodi scrupolosi di Calatrava implicano il rispetto delle condizioni economiche e funzionali di un progetto e cercano di favorire una riflessione specifica all'interno del ventaglio di possibilità tecniche disponibili. Non è un artista a briglie sciolte che va a rovistare tra gli scheletri di dinosauri in cerca di idee strampalate. Pier Luigi Nervi si è chiesto: «Perché queste forme ci soddisfano e ci toccano alla stessa stregua delle cose della natura, come i fiori, le piante, i paesaggi cui siamo abituati da innumerevoli generazioni?». Indubbiamente perché scaturiscono dalla fertile immaginazione dell'architetto-ingegnere, ma anche perché rispettano, in partenza, le forze fondamentali in gioco.

RISCOPRIRE IL PONTE

Come spiega lo stesso Calatrava, progettare un ponte implica tutta una serie di fattori molto specifici, e quello simbolico non è il meno importante. «Se si ripercorre la storia dei ponti del XIX e del XX secolo», afferma, «si è colpiti dal fatto che molti di essi sono strutture molto speciali e dense di significato. Alcuni sono rivestiti di pietra, altri decorati di leoni scolpiti o di inferriate, persino di angeli che reggono i lampioni dell'illuminazione, come nel caso del ponte Alexandre III a Parigi. Questa pratica è cessata dopo la seconda guerra mondiale. In quel periodo era urgente ricostruire in fretta centinaia di ponti in tutta Europa. Da tale necessità è nata una scuola di design esclusivamente funzionale. Un buon ponte doveva essere semplice, e soprattutto costare poco.» Calatrava

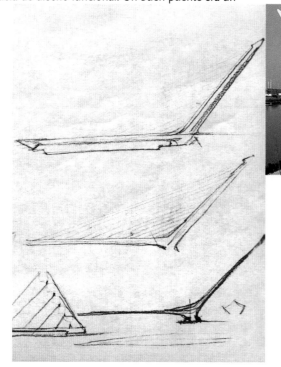

o seu título, «Torso corredor» foi buscar a sua inspiração à tensão e às forças de um corpo em movimento. Embora o uso específico que o arquitecto faz desta análise seja muito pessoal, o resultado retém algo do «estilo verdadeiro» evocado por Nervi.

De modo surpreendente, o projecto do Alamillo foi seriamente contestado antes da sua construção. Como observa Calatrava, «Alguns engenheiros tentaram demonstrar que não era sustentável ou que sairia muito mais dispendioso do que o previsto. Chegaram a contratar alguém para refazer os cálculos». Se a inveja profissional é mais frequente em arquitectura e engenharia do que em outros domínios, também é verdade que não chega muitas vezes ao conhecimento público. «Estou perfeitamente consciente», diz, «que muitos dos meus colegas sofrem mais desse género de atitude do que eu porque são ainda menos convencionais.»[16]

Fora destas controvérsias, a ponte do Alamillo parece já ter inspirado outras aplicações relativas ao conceito do pilão inclinado. O arquitecto holandês Ben van Berkel, por exemplo, que trabalhou com Calatrava durante algum tempo, acabou recentemente a ponte Erasmo (1993–1996), cuja forma possante domina agora o centro urbano de Roterdão. Apesar de o seu tabuleiro ser incrivelmente fino, esta ponte recorre a cabos traseiros, diferenciando-se do projecto sevilhano de Calatrava. Independentemente das suas qualidades técnicas, pontes deste tipo satisfazem a busca calatraviana de uma aproximação inédita e simbolizam a modernidade das cidades que embelezam.

Embora a excelência de uma ponte se imponha facilmente a qualquer pessoa, o método que conduz às suas formas é deveras complexo. «Trata-se de um processo intuitivo, isto é, um sistema baseado na síntese de diversos factores», explica o arquitecto. A descrição que faz da concepção de uma ponte merece ser citada na íntegra: «Creio que, em primeiro lugar e antes de tudo o mais, a localização da ponte não deve ser descurada. Em certos locais, por exemplo, não se poderia recorrer a um arco, porque é impossível transferir correctamente o peso até à margem. O tráfego fluvial também não deve ser desprezado, visto que o peso de uma ponte pode ser determinado pelo género de embarcações que passarão sob o seu tabuleiro. A escolha dos materiais também é essencial; a madeira, o aço ou o betão serão utilizados conforme as condições locais e os factores económicos. Estes elementos, bem como outros, induzem a certas soluções estruturais através de um processo de eliminação. É então que o tipo de ponte e o seu impacto no meio ambiente começam a tomar forma. Depois, o engenheiro deverá dedicar-se aos cálculos necessários para se assegurar que o projecto imaginado é viável. Eu construo uma maqueta que concilia a ciência matemática e a natureza, permitindo compreender o comportamento desta última. Estamos sempre em confronto com as forças da natureza», conclui.[17]

Uma das pontes mais recentes de Calatrava, a ponte para peões de Campo Volantin (Bilbau, Espanha, 1990–1997), constitui um exemplo não só da sua reflexão sobre os espaços urbanos

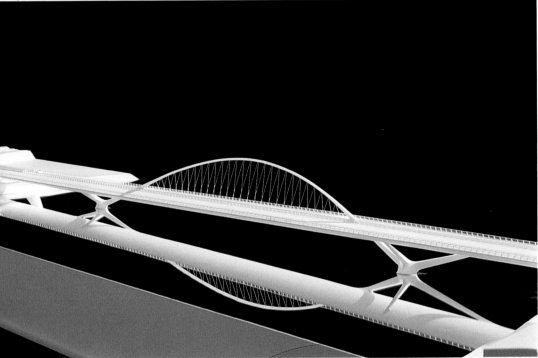

< Alamillo Bridge, Seville, Spain
> Orleans Bridge over Loire, Orleans, France

puente simple y, sobre todo, económico.» Calatrava está convencido de que esa escuela de diseño funcional de puentes está ya superada: «hoy en día hemos de redescubrir el potencial que encierran los puentes». Y menciona ejemplos de ciudades europeas como Florencia, Venecia o París para destacar el hecho de que los puentes de siglos pasados desempeñaron un papel clave para crear la imagen de esas ciudades: por su utilidad, sí, pero también por su permanencia. Para exponer su punto de vista, Santiago Calatrava llega a decir que construir un puente puede suponer un acto cultural de mayores consecuencias que construir un museo de nueva planta. «El puente es más eficaz porque es accesible para todos. Incluso una persona iletrada puede disfrutar de un puente. Un único gesto transforma la naturaleza y crea orden. Más eficaz, imposible», concluye.[13]

El éxito que ha coronado los esfuerzos de Calatrava por dar a los puentes un nuevo significado puede apreciarse muy especialmente en el Puente del Alamillo y el Viaducto de La Cartuja (Sevilla, 1987–1992). Su espectacular mástil de 142 metros tiene una inclinación de 58 grados —idéntica a la de la gran pirámide de Keops— y convierte al puente en una de las más deslumbrantes aportaciones a la Expo 92, visible desde prácticamente cualquier lugar de Sevilla. El puente está sostenido por 13 pares de cables y posee una luz de 200 metros sobre el meandro de San Jerónimo, un afluente antiguo y estancado del Guadalquivir. Independientemente de los 13 pares de cables, «el peso del mástil de acero relleno de hormigón es suficiente para servir de contrapeso al tablero, con lo que los tensores resultan superfluos»[14]. Aunque Calatrava proyectó un segundo puente, con un mástil inclinado en la dirección exactamente opuesta, como si fuera la imagen del primero reflejada en un espejo, por razones de presupuesto, el cliente —la Junta de Andalucía— se decidió a construir sólo uno y el Viaducto de La Cartuja, de 500 metros de longitud.

Al margen de sus cuadernos de bocetos, ricamente ilustrados, en los que pueden verse las ideas que le llevaron a crear esta forma

ovviamente è dell'opinione che questa scuola funzionalista abbia perso da tempo quella ragione d'essere che l'aveva giustificata nel dopoguerra. «Oggi dobbiamo riscoprire il potenziale dei ponti», dichiara, citando esempi di città europee come Firenze, Venezia o Parigi per illustrare l'idea che attraverso la loro funzione, ma anche con la loro permanenza, i ponti del passato hanno svolto un ruolo chiave nel delineare l'immagine di queste città. Per avvalorare la sua tesi Calatrava si spinge fino a sostenere che la costruzione di un ponte può essere un gesto culturale più carico di conseguenze che non la creazione di un nuovo museo. «Il ponte è più efficace», dice, «perché è accessibile a tutti. Anche un analfabeta può trovare bello un ponte. Un singolo gesto trasforma la natura e le dà ordine. Difficile essere più efficaci.»[13]

Il successo dei tentativi di Calatrava per investire di nuovo significato questa struttura architettonica è brillantemente esemplificato dal ponte di Alamillo e dal viadotto di La Cartuja (Siviglia, 1987–92). Lo spettacolare pilone alto 142 m che si erge davanti a uno degli ingressi dell'Expo '92 è inclinato di 58 gradi (come la Grande Piramide di Cheope, presso Il Cairo) ed è visibile da gran parte della città vecchia di Siviglia. Il ponte ha una luce di 200 m e supera il Meandro San Jeronimo, un ramo tutt'altro che stagnante del Guadalquivir. È sostenuto da tredici coppie di stralli, ma soprattutto «il peso del pilone riempito di calcestruzzo è sufficiente a controbilanciare l'impalcato, per cui non sono necessari stralli posteriori».[14] In origine Calatrava aveva pensato a un secondo ponte, inclinato nella direzione opposta – come un'immagine speculare del primo – che attraversasse il vicino Guadalquivir, ma motivi di budget hanno indotto il committente, la Junta dell'Andalusia, a limitarsi a un unico passaggio del fiume insieme al viadotto del Puente de la Cartuja, lungo 500 m.

Oltre che dai suoi taccuini riccamente illustrati (da cui ci si rende conto della quantità di riflessioni che hanno dato origine alla forma innovativa del pilone di Alamillo), per questo progetto Calatrava ha tratto diretta ispirazione da una sua scultura eseguita

> Alamillo Bridge, Seville, Spain

innovadora para el Puente del Alamillo, Calatrava se inspiró bastante directamente en «Torso en movimiento», una escultura que hizo él mismo en 1986, «en la que varios cubos de mármol situados unos sobre los otros se mantienen en equilibrio gracias a un cable tensado»[15]. De hecho, un buen número de los dibujos que cuelgan de las paredes de su residencia zuriquesa representan torsos en movimiento. Como su propio nombre indica, también «Torso en movimiento» se inspira en la tensión y las fuerzas de un cuerpo en movimiento. A pesar de que el uso específico que Calatrava hace de este análisis es realmente personal, el resultado recuerda en cierto modo el «estilo verdadero» de Nervi.

Sorprendentemente, el proyecto del Alamillo despertó una violenta controversia antes de construirse. Como el mismo Calatrava expone, «un buen número de ingenieros intentó probar que no se sostendría o que sería mucho más caro de lo previsto. Incluso encargaron a una persona que rehiciera los cálculos». Aun cuando los celos profesionales se encuentren tan extendidos entre los arquitectos y los ingenieros como en otras profesiones, no suelen ser de dominio público. Pero a Calatrava, esas dificultades no le quitan la paz: «estoy seguro de que muchos de mis compañeros sufren bastante más celotipias que yo, pues son todavía menos convencionales a la hora de trabajar»[16].

En este contexto habría que indicar que el Puente del Alamillo, pese a la controversia que despertó, ya ha inspirado otras aplicaciones del mástil inclinado. El arquitecto holandés Ben van Berkel, por ejemplo, quien trabajó durante cierto tiempo con Calatrava, terminó recientemente el Puente de Erasmo en Rotterdam (1993–1996), cuya poderosa silueta impone su impronta al paisaje urbano de esta ciudad. Aunque el tablero es extraordinariamente fino, este arquitecto empleó tensores, lo que le diferencia del puente sevillano de Calatrava. Independientemente de su calidad técnica, proyectos como éste manifiestan claramente el empeño de Calatrava por encontrar un nuevo diseño como símbolo de la modernidad de la ciudad.

nel 1986, il *Torso in corsa*, «dove una pila inclinata di cubi di marmo è tenuta in equilibrio da un filo metallico in tensione».[15] Molti dei disegni appesi alle pareti della casa zurighese dell'architetto rappresentano figure in movimento. *Torso in corsa* è chiaramente ispirato, come sottintende il titolo, alla tensione e alle forze di un corpo lanciato in avanti. Sebbene l'uso specifico che Calatrava fa di questa analisi sia molto personale, il risultato rinvia un po' allo «stile veritiero» descritto da Nervi.

Curiosamente il progetto dell'Alamillo è stato oggetto di severe contestazioni prima della sua realizzazione. Calatrava racconta: «Parecchi ingegneri hanno cercato di dimostrare che il ponte non avrebbe tenuto, o che avrebbe comportato costi più elevati del previsto. Hanno persino incaricato qualcuno di rifare i calcoli». Certo, la gelosia professionale è altrettanto comune nell'architettura e nell'ingegneria che negli altri settori, ma non succede spesso che diventi una questione di dominio pubblico. Calatrava si comporta con filosofia di fronte a queste difficoltà. «Sono del tutto consapevole», ammette, «che molti dei miei colleghi risentono maggiormente di questo tipo di atteggiamenti, perché loro sono ancora meno convenzionali.»[16]

Occorre notare che, nonostante i suoi aspetti controversi, il ponte di Alamillo pare aver già ispirato altre significative applicazioni del concetto del pilone inclinato. L'architetto olandese Ben van Berkel, per esempio, che per qualche tempo ha lavorato con Calatrava, ha di recente completato a Rotterdam il ponte Erasmus (1993–96), il cui possente profilo contrassegna il paesaggio urbano del centro della città. Pur con un impalcato notevolmente sottile, a differenza della struttura di Calatrava per Siviglia, questo ponte si avvale di stralli posteriori. A prescindere dalle qualità tecniche, è chiaro che ponti come questi sono in linea con l'approccio innovativo propugnato da Calatrava, in quanto simboli della modernità delle città che essi abbelliscono.

Se la bellezza di un ponte può essere facilmente percepita anche dai «non addetti ai lavori», il metodo che porta alla creazione di

periféricos ou industriais, como de um proficiente exercício de engenharia que desabrochou de uma forma invulgar. Atravessar o rio de Bilbau para ligar o centro da cidade a uma zona comercial em declínio denominada Urbitarte, exige recorrer ao princípio do arco inclinado, que Calatrava aplicou pela primeira vez em 1988 no seu projecto não realizado de uma nova ponte sobre o Sena, a qual deveria ligar a estação de Lyon à de Austerlitz. Aqui, um arco parabólico inclinado, com uma abertura de 71 m, suporta uma passadeira encurvada de recorte surpreendente. No entanto, a curva é mais que um efeito estético. Como esclarece Sergio Polano, «A tensão criada nos pontos de suspensão das vigas pela excentricidade do peso é contrabalançada graças à contracurva da passadeira, transferindo assim o peso para os alicerces em betão» e conferindo ao conjunto o aspecto de «um pêndulo em movimento suspenso». Repetindo o caso da ponte do Alamillo, um espectacular sistema de iluminação perpetua o impacto estético da ponte durante a noite.

A LINGUAGEM DAS TORRES

Permanece por confirmar se as teorias de Calatrava sobre o impacto positivo da ponte conseguirão modificar a atmosfera desta zona de Bilbau, mas é certo que a cidade aposta no investimento numa arquitectura de qualidade. Uma nova linha metropolitana, concebida por Sir Norman Foster, e o Museu Guggenheim de Bilbau , concluído recentemente por Frank Gehry, ilustram bem a ambição dessa grande cidade do norte de Espanha. A intervenção de Calatrava também não se limita à ponte para peões de Campo Volatin. Foi também incumbido do alargamento do aeroporto, tendo de criar para o efeito um novo terminal e uma nova torre de controlo. A torre do aeroporto de Sondica, com 42 m de altura e que contém equipamento tecnológico, escritórios e a actual sala de controlo em forma de tronco cónico invertido, oferecendo uma vista panorâmica, ilustra outro centro de interesse de Calatrava: as estruturas elevadas. O mais conhecido dos seus projectos nesse domínio é com certeza a torre de comunicações de Montjuic (Barcelona, 1989–1992). Construída aquando dos Jogos Olímpicos, tem cerca de 130 m de altura e destaca-se pela sua constituição inclinada, tendo sido comparada a um dardo em lançamento. Todavia, como é hábito, a ideia de Calatrava é assaz inesperada. Os seus desenhos preparatórios demonstram que a forma vertical foi inspirada por uma figura humana ajoelhada em posição de oferenda. De igual modo, o plano da torre poderá parecer ter sido sugerido por símbolos maçónicos, como o compasso. O arquitecto insiste em afirmar que esta impressão está incorrecta, e que o olho humano foi uma vez mais a fonte de inspiração. O olho, podemos adiantar, também é um símbolo maçónico, mas a concepção e o conteúdo da Torre de Montjuic estão recheados de significados múltiplos, tendo a sua técnica de construção gerado uma forma dinâmica estonteante. Como comenta o catálogo da exposição de 1993, «Simbolicamente, a torre refere-se ao evento ritual dos Jogos Olímpicos. A sua forma singular não contraria as leis da

> Sculpture V, Running Torso
> Bauschänzli Restaurant, Zurich

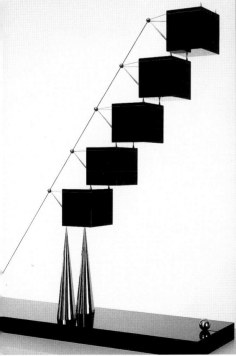

Aunque cualquier persona pueda apreciar fácilmente la belleza de un puente, el método que conduce a esas formas es realmente complejo. «Se trata de un proceso intuitivo, es decir el sistema resultante de la síntesis de varios factores», explica Calatrava. Su descripción del proyecto de un puente merece ser citada íntegramente: «Creo que lo primero y más importante a tener en cuenta es la localización del puente. Por ejemplo, en algunos lugares no se puede emplear un arco, porque no es factible transportar las cargas a las orillas de un modo apropiado. Además, hay que tener en cuenta el tráfico fluvial: la altura del puente puede quedar determinada por el tipo de barcos que han de pasar por debajo de él. E igualmente esencial es la selección de los materiales; el uso de madera, acero u hormigón dependerá de las circunstancias locales y del presupuesto. Estos y otros criterios llevan, a través de un proceso de eliminación, a ciertas soluciones estructurales factibles. Es entonces cuando comienzan a darle forma no sólo el tipo de puente mismo, sino también el impacto que causa sobre el entorno. Y entonces también ha llegado el momento en que el ingeniero ha de hacer los cálculos necesarios para estar seguro de que el diseño que ha imaginado es realmente viable. Yo desarrollo un modelo que une las matemáticas con la naturaleza y que permite comprender el comportamiento de ésta. Siempre nos enfrentamos con las fuerzas de la naturaleza.»[17]

Uno de los puentes recientemente construidos por Calatrava es la Pasarela del Campo Volantín (Bilbao, 1990–1997), no sólo paradigma de sus reflexiones sobre los espacios urbanos periféricos o industriales, sino también un extraordinario ejercicio de ingeniería que conduce a una forma inesperada. Atraviesa la ría de Bilbao, uniendo el casco urbano con la degradada zona industrial de Urbitarte; la pasarela se basa en el principio del arco inclinado, que Calatrava empleó por primera vez en un proyecto de 1988 (que no llegó a construirse) para un puente del Sena, entre el 12° y el 13° arrondissement, y que habría unido la Estación de Lyón con la de Austerlitz. En Bilbao, un arco parabólico inclinado de 71 metros

queste forme è naturalmente assai complesso. «È un processo intuitivo, si tratta cioè di un sistema imperniato sulla sintesi di una serie di fattori», spiega l'architetto. La sua descrizione della fase progettuale di un ponte merita di essere citata per esteso: «Credo che prima di tutto occorra prendere in considerazione l'ubicazione. In certi siti, per esempio, non si può utilizzare l'arco perché non è possibile trasferire i carichi sulle rive in modo corretto. Bisogna poi tener conto del traffico fluviale. L'altezza di un ponte può infatti essere determinata dal tipo di imbarcazioni che devono passare sotto il suo impalcato. Anche la scelta dei materiali è di primaria importanza: legno, acciaio o cemento armato devono essere impiegati a seconda delle circostanze locali e dei fattori economici. Attraverso un processo di eliminazione, questi e altri elementi determinano le soluzioni strutturali possibili. È solo a questo punto che il ponte, in base al tipo di struttura prescelto e considerato il suo impatto ambientale, comincia ad assumere una forma. Spetta allora all'ingegnere fare i calcoli necessari per assicurarsi che il disegno da lui concepito sia davvero attuabile. Creo dunque un modello che collega la scienza matematica alla natura e permette la comprensione del comportamento di quest'ultima. Ci troviamo sempre a confronto con le forze della natura».[17]

Una recente realizzazione di Calatrava, il ponte pedonale di Campo Volantin (Bilbao, Spagna, 1990–97), è esemplare delle sue idee sugli spazi urbani periferici o industriali, oltre a essere un sofisticato esercizio di ingegneria sfociato in una forma singolare. La passerella, che oltrepassa il fiume Nervión per collegare il centro della città con una zona commerciale dismessa denominata Urbitarte, sfrutta il principio dell'arco inclinato applicato per la prima volta da Calatrava in un progetto del 1988 (non realizzato) per un nuovo ponte sulla Senna, tra il XII e il XIII arrondissement, inteso a collegare la Gare de Lyon alla Gare d'Austerlitz. A Bilbao, un arco parabolico inclinato con una luce di 71 m sostiene una passerella curva dal design mozzafiato.

estática, pois o centro de gravidade na base coincide com a vertical resultante do seu peso morto. A inclinação corresponde ao ângulo do solstício de Verão em Barcelona, e actua como um relógio solar conforme o sol atravessa a plataforma circular na base das escadas. Estas características evocam a existência de duas grandes avenidas em Barcelona, La Meridiana e El Paralelo, ecos da vocação *avant-garde* da cidade e referências ao progresso técnico da época».[19]

Uma outra torre de Calatrava deve ser citada pelo seu desenho espectacular, ainda que nunca venha a ser construída. Esta faria parte de um conjunto, compreendendo um planetário, um museu e um teatro de ópera, sobre o qual o arquitecto trabalha ainda para a sua terra natal, Valência. A torre, vencedora de um concurso organizado em 1991 pela «Generalitat Valenciana no âmbito do seu projecto "Cidade das Ciências", destinado a reabilitar uma zona periférica a leste de Valência, entre o rio Turia e uma auto-estrada», seria o elemento simbólico mais visível desse complexo. Como escreveu Sergio Polano, «Elevando-se a partir de uma base triangular com faces convexas a uma altura de 382 m, a torre situa-se no topo de uma praça irregular com um pátio central circular... elevadores de vidro ascendem até à plataforma panorâmica localizada aproximadamente a meio da torre (172 m)... Os três "pés" que formam a base distinguem-se pelo seu curioso plano em gota (um triângulo isósceles estreito, de base semicircular), implantados simetricamente num triângulo equilátero, o qual está, por sua vez, inscrito num círculo com 41 m de raio. Construídos em betão armado e revestidos de vidro e aço, os três elementos da base afunilam à medida que trepam em direcção ao centro simétrico da estrutura, encontrando-se a uma altura de 162 m para formar a plataforma em estrela que suporta a flecha fusiforme da torre de telecomunicações.»[20]

MUNDOS A CONSTRUIR

Alguns dos projectos mais interessantes de Calatrava, como a torre de Valência, nunca serão construídos. Este facto não é raro, em particular para aqueles arquitectos que, como ele, participam tão activamente em concursos. Contudo, é indubitável que os seus insólitos trabalhos granjeiem mais críticas que outros. «Da minha parte», diz, «expresso sempre ao cliente o meu desejo de ir mais longe através de razões bastante sólidas. Não é aí que ocorrem os problemas. Para a comunidade dos engenheiros ou dos arquitectos, alguns dos meus projectos levantaram verdadeiros escândalos. Acusaram-me de ter cometido erros de cálculo graves, o que parece infundado se considerarmos aquilo que já construí. Os arquitectos são das pessoas mais conservadoras que existem. É verdade que os meus melhores projectos não foram construídos, mas julgo que estas situações, deveras frustrantes, acompanham forçosamente as pesquisas mais inovadoras.»

O maior e, talvez, o mais controverso dos projectos não realizados de Calatrava é a sua concepção do novo Parlamento alemão, ou Reichstag (Berlim, Alemanha, 1992). Este edifício sólido, cuja

< The Sculpture Bird
> Palacio de las Artes, Valencia, Spain

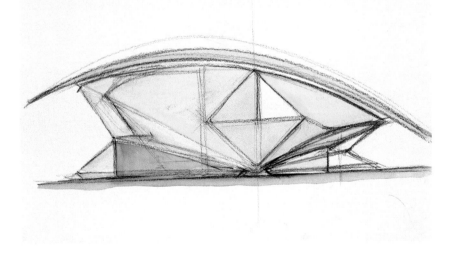

sostiene una pasarela curva con un diseño sumamente sugestivo. Pero esta curva es más que una licencia artística. Como expone Sergio Polano, «la torsión desarrollada en los puntos de suspensión de los apoyos por la situación excéntrica de las pesos es compensada por la contracurva de la pasarela que transfiere la resultante de las cargas a los cimientos en hormigón del puente». El conjunto recuerda «un péndulo en movimiento suspendido»[18]. Al igual que en el caso del Puente del Alamillo, un espectacular sistema de iluminación acentúa el efecto que causa el puente de noche, completando así el proyecto.

LA RETORICA DE LAS TORRES

Todavía está por ver si, como afirma la teoría de Calatrava, el puente es capaz de cambiar la atmósfera de una ciudad o la de este barrio de Bilbao. En cualquier caso, la administración municipal cree que merece la pena invertir en una arquitectura de calidad. La nueva línea de metro, diseñada por Sir Norman Foster, y el Museo Guggenheim de Bilbao, recientemente construido por Frank O. Gehry, evidencian las ambiciones de esta ciudad vasca. Pero la intervención de Santiago Calatrava no se limitó al Puente del Campo Volantín: también se le encargó la ampliación del Aeropuerto de Sondica, al que se añadirá una nueva terminal y una Torre de Control. La Torre de Control (1993–1996), de 42 metros de altura, que alberga las instalaciones técnicas, las oficinas y la sala de control propiamente dicha, adopta la forma de un cono truncado e invertido, ofreciendo una vista panorámica; es un buen ejemplo de otro de los campos de interés de Calatrava: las torres.

El más conocido de esos proyectos es, sin duda, la Torre de Comunicaciones de Montjuic (Barcelona, 1989–1992), construida con ocasión de los Juegos Olímpicos que se celebraron en la ciudad condal. Con sus 130 metros de altura y su fuste inclinado, se la ha comparado con una jabalina; pero como es usual en las obras de Calatrava, también en este caso se sigue un planteamiento fuera de lo común. Sus dibujos preparatorios revelan que este diseño vertical

Tuttavia quella curva non è una mera licenza artistica. Come spiega Sergio Polano, «la torsione sviluppata nei punti di sospensione delle lame dall'eccentricità del peso sulla passerella è bilanciata dalla curvatura della trave scatolare che trasferisce la risultante dei carichi di torsione alle fondazioni in calcestruzzo del ponte», e il tutto suggerisce «un pendolo sospeso nel suo moto».[18] Come nel caso del ponte di Alamillo, il progetto è completato da uno spettacolare sistema d'illuminazione, che accentua l'impatto del ponte in notturna.

IL LINGUAGGIO DELLE TORRI

Resta da vedere se le teorie di Calatrava circa l'impatto positivo di un ponte riusciranno a cambiare l'atmosfera di questo quartiere di Bilbao. La città è comunque convinta che valga la pena investire nella buona architettura e nel design di qualità. Una nuova linea della metropolitana progettata da Sir Norman Foster e il Guggenheim Bilbao Museum recentemente completato da Frank O. Gehry testimoniano delle ambizioni di questa città del Nord della Spagna. Lo stesso intervento di Calatrava non si limita al ponte pedonale di Campo Volantin. Gli è stato anche affidato l'ampliamento dell'aeroporto con l'aggiunta di un nuovo terminal e di una torre di controllo. Alta 42 m, a forma di tronco di cono capovolto, la torre dell'aeroporto di Sondica (1993–96) – che ospita attrezzature tecniche, uffici e la sala di controllo vera e propria, da cui si gode un'ampia vista panoramica – illustra un altro centro d'interesse di Calatrava: le costruzioni alte. Il più famoso dei suoi progetti in questo ambito è sicuramente la torre delle telecomunicazioni di Montjuic (Barcellona, 1989–92), realizzata in occasione delle Olimpiadi del 1992. Alta circa 130 m, a fusto inclinato, è stata paragonata a un giavellotto scagliato, ma anche in questo caso l'approccio scelto da Calatrava è tutt'altro che scontato. Dai disegni risulta chiaro che la sagoma verticale è desunta da una figura inginocchiata mentre porge un'offerta. In modo analogo, la pianta della torre sembrerebbe

construção foi decidida em 28 de Março de 1871, na extremidade leste da Königsplatz, já levantou vários problemas arquitectónicos no passado. O arquitecto vencedor do concurso de 1871, Friedrich Bohnstedt, foi afastado para dar lugar a Paul Wallot uma década mais tarde. O próprio Wallot abandonou o projecto anos antes da epígrafe proposta, «Dem deutschen Volke» (Ao povo alemão), ter sido gravada no edifício. A agonia do Reichstag, desde o incêndio de 1933 à chegada do Exército Vermelho, é bem conhecida. A renovação e conversão do edifício, destinado a tornar-se a nova sede do Bundestag, foi decidida em 31 de Outubro de 1991, e o concurso foi anunciado em 26 de Junho de 1992. Três arquitectos – Calatrava, o holandês Pi de Bruijn e Sir Norman Foster – destacaram-se durante o processo de selecção. Foster propusera um imenso dossel que cobriria não só o edifício, como as imediações mais próximas. O projecto de Calatrava, pelo contrário, procurava dotar o edifício de uma nova cúpula para substituir a estrutura original em alvenaria, a qual fora demolida após a Segunda Guerra Mundial. Os seus desenhos e maquetas demonstravam que esta cúpula teria sido extremamente ligeira, «Imaginei uma concha muito fina, constituída a partir de uma membrana de perfis leves em aço, gerando um efeito de tensão, suportada a partir do interior por uma rede de cabos. A minha ideia era produzir, de entre as construções possíveis, a mais fina, a mais ligeira e a mais transparente, recorrendo aos meios mais modernos.» Dentro da cúpula, elementos em forma de pétala abrir-se-iam ou fechar-se-iam como uma flor, de modo a proporcionar a entrada de luz solar na sala do Parlamento logo abaixo. Esta cúpula desencadeou a controvérsia que Michel Cullen resumiu como se segue: «No fim de Abril de 1993, foi solicitado aos três arquitectos que refizessem os seus projectos até ao dia 14 de Junho, incorporando novas especificações, as quais incluíam o uso do espaço no bloco Dorotheen a leste, e a orientação da sala do parlamento face ao edifício presidencial também a leste, duas ideias propostas originalmente por Calatrava. Este foi o único a desenvolver o seu projecto original; os outros dois surgiram com soluções inteiramente diferentes. Não foi necessário proceder a uma nova sessão do júri. A apresentação dos trabalhos a 17 de Junho não foi pública, e parece que não se conservaram quaisquer registos. Em 19 de Junho, tomou-se conhecimento pela imprensa berlinense que fora tomada uma decisão favorável a Sir Norman Foster. Em 21 de Junho, a Comissão para o Urbanismo do Conselho dos Anciãos decidiu, sem ter pedido a opinião de um perito, entregar a obra ao arquitecto inglês. No dia 1 de Julho, com a presença de Rita Süssmuth, presidente parlamentar, foi decidido pedir a Foster não só para incutir uma maior exactidão aos planos, mas também, em concordância com a proposta de Calatrava, reconsiderar a concepção de uma cúpula.»[21] O projecto revisto por Foster foi aprovado pelo Bundestag em 29 de Junho de 1994, e Santiago Calatrava fez saber imediatamente que o projecto inglês se assemelhava demasiado à sua própria concepção, ataque que Foster rejeitou em absoluto.

Outro projecto seu bastante interessante, mas não realizado, foi a proposta vencedora do concurso

se inspira en una figura humana arrodillada para hacer una ofrenda. Al mismo tiempo, la planta hace pensar en símbolos masónicos como el compás. Pero Santiago Calatrava insiste en que esta apreciación es incorrecta, y hace hincapié en que fue el ojo humano lo que le inspiró. Naturalmente que el ojo también es un símbolo masónico, pero la concepción y el contenido de la Torre de Montjuic tienen evidentemente diversos significados, del mismo modo que su técnica de construcción creó una forma extraordinariamente dinámica. Como explica el catálogo de la exposición que se organizó en 1993: «Simbólicamente, la torre se refiere al ritual de los Juegos Olímpicos. Su singular forma no contradice las leyes de la estática, porque el centro de gravedad coincide, en la base, con la vertical resultante de su peso muerto. La inclinación del fuste coincide con el ángulo del solsticio de verano en Barcelona; el fuste actúa como un reloj de sol, proyectando su sombra sobre la plataforma circular que se encuentra al pie de las escaleras. Estas características recuerdan la existencia de dos importantes avenidas en Barcelona: La Meridiana y El Paralelo, que denotan la vocación vanguardista de esta ciudad y remiten a los avances técnicos de ese periodo.»[19]

Aunque no será construida, aún es digna de mención otra torre diseñada por Calatrava, por su espectacular diseño. Originalmente, estaba pensada como parte de un conjunto, con un planetario, un museo y una ópera, que está proyectando para su ciudad natal, Valencia. La torre, con la que en 1991 ganó el concurso organizado por la Generalitat Valenciana para la Ciudad de las Ciencias «con el objeto de rehabilitar una zona periférica al este de Valencia, entre el Turia y la autopista», estaba prevista como el elemento simbólico más destacado del complejo. Sergio Polano la ha descrito de la siguiente manera: «La torre se sitúa en un área triangular asimétrica de 41.820 metros cuadrados. Con una altura de 382 metros, surge un zócalo de planta triangular con lados curvos, que define al Oeste una plaza irregular de acceso, articulado en varios niveles a través de un patio circular (...) ascensores panorámicos llevan al mirador situado

a prima vista ispirarsi a simboli massonici quali la bussola. Santiago Calatrava insiste che questa particolare impressione non è corretta e che ancora una volta è l'occhio umano a ispirarlo. Naturalmente anche l'occhio è un simbolo massonico, ma la concezione e il contenuto della torre di Montjuic presentano tutta una serie di sfaccettature, proprio come la tecnica di costruzione impiegata, che ha generato una forma sorprendentemente dinamica. Come spiega il catalogo dell'esposizione del 1993: «Simbolicamente, la torre rinvia all'evento rituale delle Olimpiadi. La sua forma singolare non contraddice le leggi della statica, perché il centro di gravità coincide alla base con la verticale risultante dal suo carico fisso. L'inclinazione coincide con l'angolo del solstizio d'estate a Barcellona e il fusto funziona come lo gnomone di una meridiana quando il sole proietta la sua luce sulla piattaforma circolare ai piedi delle scale. Queste caratteristiche richiamano l'esistenza di due grandi viali di Barcellona, La Meridiana ed El Paralelo, testimonianze della vocazione all'avanguardia di questa città e punto di riferimento dei progressi tecnici dell'epoca».[19]

Anche se non verrà costruita, un'altra torre disegnata da Calatrava merita di essere menzionata per la sua concezione spettacolare, e anche perché doveva far parte di un complesso comprendente un planetario, un museo e un teatro dell'opera per la sua città natale di Valencia, progetto cui l'architetto sta tuttora lavorando. La torre, per la quale ha vinto nel 1991 un concorso organizzato dalla «Generalitat Valenciana come parte del progetto della Città delle Scienze, volto a riabilitare un'area periferica a est di Valencia, collocata tra il fiume Turia e l'autostrada», doveva essere l'elemento simbolico più visibile di questo complesso. Come ha scritto Sergio Polano: «Alta 382 m, [la torre] sorge su un basamento a pianta triangolare dai lati curvi, che definisce a ovest una piazza irregolare d'ingresso, articolato in più livelli attraverso una corte circolare [...] Ascensori panoramici [portano] al belvedere a quota 172 m [...] Tre "zampe" incastrate nelle

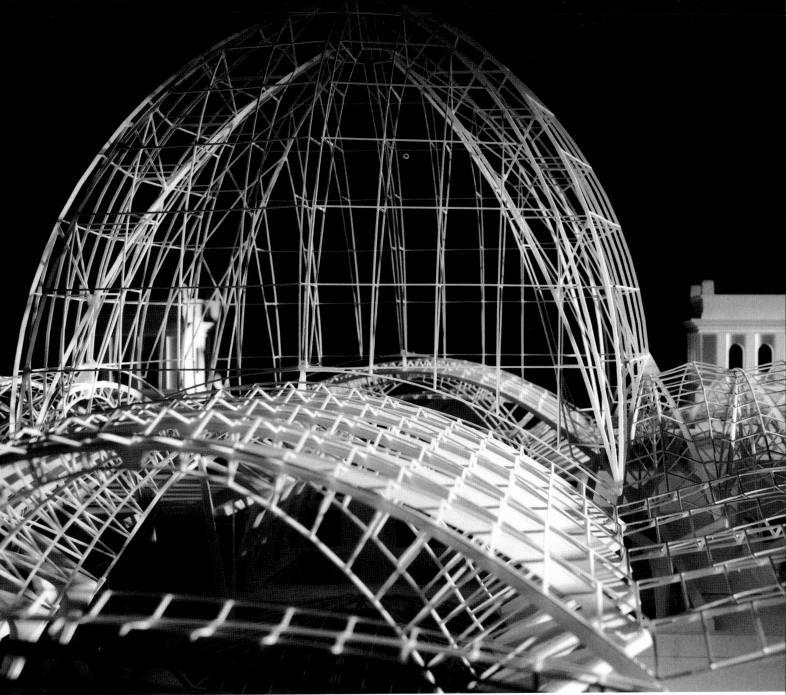

> Reichstag Conversion Competition, Berlin, Germany

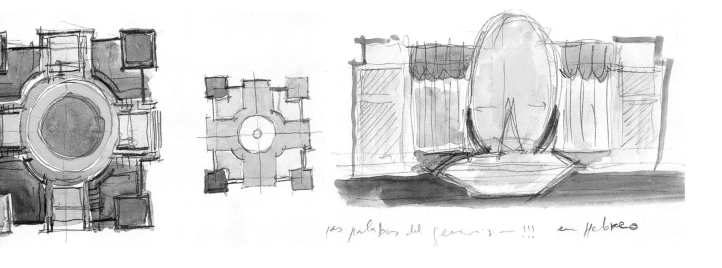

las palabras del genesis — !!! en Hebreo

a 172 metros de altura y sistemas de escaleras a los niveles inferiores. Tres 'patas' embutidas en los cimientos y en el zócalo, con sección de gota (un triángulo isósceles de base semicircular), están dispuestas simétricamente dentro de un triángulo equilátero, inscrito en una circunferencia de 41 metros de radio. Construidas en hormigón armado y revestidas de placas de acero y cristal, se elevan ahusándose hacia el centro de simetría de la estructura (...) y se unen a 162 metros de altura para formar una planta estrellada que sirve de apoyo a la aguja de telecomunicaciones.»[20]

MUNDOS A LA ESPERA DE SU CONSTRUCCION

Algunos de los proyectos más interesantes de Santiago Calatrava, como la Torre de Valencia, no se construirán nunca. Este hecho no es tan inusual, especialmente para los arquitectos que participan tan activamente en concursos como él. Y, sin embargo, los proyectos de Calatrava que se salen de lo corriente están expuestos a mayor crítica que otros. «Si juzgo las cosas desde mi punto de vista —dice— suelo presentar al cliente, con explicaciones sólidas, mi deseo de ir más allá de lo que normalmente se espera. Por lo tanto, el problema no está aquí. Por el contrario, en el gremio de arquitectos e ingenieros, algunos de mis proyectos han producido verdaderos escándalos. Algunos se rasgaron las vestiduras y me acusaron de equivocarme en los cálculos... lo que no parece ser el caso si uno se fija en mi obra construida. Los arquitectos son de las personas más conservadoras del mundo. Es cierto que los mejores proyectos que yo he realizado nunca serán construidos, pero admito que esa situación, ciertamente frustrante, forma parte necesariamente de una investigación innovadora.»

El mayor, y en cierto modo el más controvertido, de los proyectos no construidos de Santiago Calatrava es su propuesta para la instalación del Parlamento Alemán en el Reichstag (Berlín, 1992). Es importante recordar que el Reichstag, cuya construcción al este de la Königsplatz se decidió el 28 de marzo de 1871, en el pasado causó problemas arquitectónicos más de una vez. El arquitecto que ganó el concurso

fondazioni e nel basamento, con sezione a goccia (un triangolo isoscele a base semicircolare), sono disposte simmetricamente all'interno di un triangolo equilatero, inscritto in una circonferenza di 41 m di raggio, costruite in cemento armato e rivestite di lastre d'acciaio e vetro, si innalzano rastremandosi verso il centro di simmetria della struttura, [...] e si uniscono a quota 162 m a formare una pianta stellare, di supporto alla guglia delle telecomunicazioni».[20]

MONDI CHE ATTENDONO DI ESSERE COSTRUITI

Un certo numero dei progetti più interessanti di Santiago Calatrava, fra cui la torre di Valencia, non verranno mai realizzati. Non è un fatto insolito, soprattutto per architetti che, come lui, partecipano così attivamente ai concorsi, ma può darsi che le sue imprevedibili concezioni attirino più critiche di altre. «Se giudico le cose dal mio punto di vista», spiega Calatrava, «devo dire che giustifico sempre presso il cliente, fornendo validi argomenti, il mio desiderio di andare oltre quello che ci si aspetta da me. Non è qui che nascono i problemi. È invece a fronte della comunità degli ingegneri o degli architetti che certi miei progetti hanno scatenato dei veri e propri scandali. Sono stato accusato di assurdi errori di calcolo, il che non pare essere assolutamente il caso se si considera quello che ho già costruito. Gli architetti sono fra le persone più conservatrici in circolazione. È vero che i miei migliori progetti non sono stati costruiti, ma trovo che questo genere di esperienze, per quanto frustranti, siano una componente necessaria della ricerca innovativa.»

Il più vasto, e per certi versi più contestato, fra i progetti non costruiti di Santiago Calatrava è la sua proposta per il nuovo Parlamento tedesco presso il Reichstag (Berlino, Germania, 1992). A questo proposito occorre ricordare che la costruzione del Reichstag, sul lato orientale della Königsplatz, decisa il 28 marzo 1871, già in passato ha sollevato parecchi problemi dal punto di vista architettonico. Il vincitore del concorso del 1871, Friedrich

original, Friedrich Bohnstedt, fue descartado una década más tarde en favor de Paul Wallot. Y Wallot, a su vez, abandonó el proyecto años antes de que se colocara en el frontón del edificio la inscripción que él propuso: «Dem deutschen Volke» (Al pueblo alemán).

Es conocida la historia agónica del Reichstag desde el incendio de 1933 hasta que fue tomado por el Ejército Rojo. El 31 de octubre de 1991 se decidió la rehabilitación y transformación del Reichstag en la sede del Bundestag. El concurso se publicó el 26 de junio de 1992. En una primera fase fueron seleccionados los proyectos de tres arquitectos —Calatrava, el holandés Pi De Bruijn y Norman Foster—. Este último presentó un proyecto con un dosel sobredimensionado, que habría cubierto no sólo el Reichstag, sino también el entorno inmediato. Por el contrario, el proyecto de Calatrava se centraba en cubrir de nuevo el Reichstag con una cúpula para reemplazar la original de mampostería, que quedó destruida en la Segunda Guerra Mundial. Como muestran sus maquetas y bocetos, habría sido una cúpula extremadamente ligera. Dejemos que lo explique con sus propias palabras: «Ideé una cubierta muy fina, con una membrana constituida por perfiles de acero ligero, que parecía estar tensada por una red de cables en su interior. Mi intención era hacer la construcción lo más ligera, más fina y más transparente posible, empleando los medios más modernos posibles.» En su interior, la cúpula tenía elementos similares a pétalos que se abrían y cerraban, como en una flor, para difundir la luz del día a la Sala de Plenos situada debajo.

Precisamente esta cúpula desencadenó la controversia que Michael Cullen ha resumido de la siguiente manera: «A finales de abril de 1993, se requirió a los tres arquitectos a que reelaboraran sus proyectos, hasta el 14 de junio, incorporando nuevas especificaciones. Estas incluían la utilización del espacio en el Dorotheenblock, al este, y la orientación de la Sala de Plenos hacia la sede del Presidente de la República, igualmente al este... dos ideas que Calatrava ya había previsto en su primer proyecto. Y Calatrava fue el único de los tres que realmente remodeló su anterior

Bohnstedt, venne «licenziato» dieci anni dopo per essere sostituito da Paul Wallot. Lo stesso Wallot abbandonò il progetto anni prima che il motto da lui proposto, «Dem deutschen Volke» (Al popolo tedesco), fosse finalmente inciso sull'edificio. L'agonia del Reichstag, dall'incendio del 1933 all'arrivo dell'Armata Rossa, è nota. La ristrutturazione dell'edificio per convertirlo nella sede del Bundestag è stata decisa il 31 ottobre 1991 e il relativo concorso è stato indetto il 26 giugno 1992. Nella fase di selezione si sono distinti tre architetti: Calatrava, l'olandese Pi de Bruijn e Sir Norman Foster. Foster aveva proposto una singolare calotta, immensa, che avrebbe coperto non soltanto il Reichstag ma anche le sue immediate vicinanze. Il progetto di Calatrava, al contrario, mirava a coronare l'edificio con una cupola per rimpiazzare la struttura originale in muratura demolita dopo la seconda guerra mondiale. Come si vede dai disegni e dai modelli di Calatrava, questa cupola sarebbe stata estremamente leggera. «Ho pensato a una copertura sottile», racconta Calatrava, «realizzata con una membrana di profilati leggeri d'acciaio, tenuta in tensione da una rete interna di cavi. La mia intenzione era creare la costruzione più leggera, più sottile e più trasparente possibile, servendomi dei mezzi più moderni.» All'interno della cupola, elementi simili ai petali di un fiore si sarebbero aperti o chiusi per lasciar entrare la luce del giorno nella sala dell'assemblea plenaria sottostante. È a questo punto che, durante la selezione, sono scoppiate le polemiche. Michael Cullen ha riassunto l'accaduto come segue: «Alla fine dell'aprile 1993 fu chiesto ai tre architetti di rielaborare i loro progetti entro il 14 giugno, accludendo le specifiche di rettifica. Queste nuove specifiche includevano l'utilizzo dello spazio dell'adiacente Dorotheenblock, a est, e l'orientamento della sala assembleare rispetto all'edificio presidenziale, anch'esso sul lato orientale: due idee già proposte da Calatrava. Quest'ultimo fu l'unico dei tre a intervenire sul progetto originale, sviluppandolo secondo le richieste; gli altri due concorrenti fornirono invece delle soluzioni radicalmente diverse. Una nuova sessione della giuria non fu ritenuta necessaria. La presentazione dei

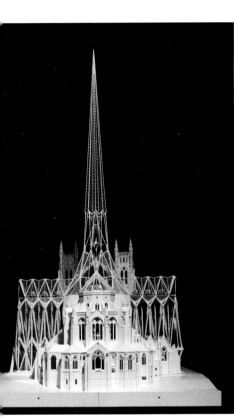

para a Catedral de St. John the Divine (Nova Iorque, EUA, 1991). Construído em 1892 e 'goticizado' em 1911, este monumento de Manhattan é a maior igreja neogótica do mundo. A partir de elementos estruturais de aparência orgânica, Calatrava propusera a criação de uma espécie de bio-refúgio a 55 m abaixo do solo do santuário. Os planos das igrejas góticas baseavam-se na metáfora da árvore, e o arquitecto repescou esta ideia para criar um jardim no céu, o qual corresponderia à folhagem da tal árvore metafórica, mas evocando também o jardim do Éden. Mais uma vez abundantemente ilustrado pelos seus desenhos e maquetas, este projecto realça a busca de uma significação mais profunda para a arquitectura moderna. Aqui, como na maior parte dos projectos calatravianos, encontramos uma pesquisa não só ao nível das soluções funcionais, como das referências dotadas de sentido. Estas nem sempre são evidentes, pois baseiam-se na imaginação pessoal de Calatrava ou nas suas esculturas, embora manifestem uma autenticidade que justifica a sua rápida ascensão como um dos arquitectos-engenheiros mais famosos do mundo. A transgressão é um dos seus termos preferidos, sustentado pela sua própria definição da palavra, a qual implica um estudo atento e um conhecimento prático profundo, postos, por seu turno, ao serviço do desejo de criar formas surpreendentes. Nas suas mãos, as pontes e as estações ganharam uma nova vida, deixando para trás o árido funcionalismo típico do período de reconstrução do pós-guerra. Progredindo a partir de esboços e esculturas, Calatrava trabalha na fronteira de um domínio muito particular da criação, onde a arte, a arquitectura e a engenharia se encontram. Em 1877, as palavras de Davioud, que faziam referência ao pacto entre o arquitecto e o engenheiro, o qual, dizia, «...nunca se tornará realidade, completo e frutífero até que o engenheiro, o artista e o cientista se fundam numa só pessoa», poderiam ser simplesmente a descrição do talento nato de Santiago Calatrava.

1 Entrevista com Santiago Calatrava, Paris, Novembro de 1995.
2 Giedeon, Sigfried: *Space, Time and Architecture*, Harvard University Press, Cambridge, MA, 5ffi Edição, 1976.
3 McQuaid, Matilda: *Santiago Calatrava, Structure and Expression*, The Museum of Modern Art, Nova Iorque, 1993.
4 Ibid.
5 Entrevista com Santiago Calatrava, Zurique, Junho de 1997.
6 Ibid.
7 Nervi, Pier Luigi: *Aesthetics and Tecnology in Building, The Charles Eliot Norton Lectures, 1961-1962*, Harvard University Press, Cambridge, MA, 1965.
8 Entrevista com Santiago Calatrava, Zurique, Junho de 1997.
9 Ibid.
10 Ibid.
11 Ibid.
12 Ibid.
13 Ibid.
14 Sharp, Dennis (ed.): *Santiago Calatrava*, Architectural Monographs n° 46, Academy Editions, Londres, 1996.
15 Ibid.
16 Entrevista com Santiago Calatrava, Zurique, Junho de 1997.
17 Ibid.
18 Polano, Sergio: Santiago Calatrava, Complete Works, Gingko, Electa, Milão, 1996.
19 *Santiago Calatrava, 1983-93*, Catalogo de la exposicion antologica en la Lonja de Valencia del 31 de Mayo al 30 de Junio de 1993, El Croquis Editorial, Madrid, 1993.
20 Polano, Sergio: *Santiago Calatrava*, Complete Works, Gingko, Electa, Milão, 1996.
21 Cullen, Michael: *Calatrava Berlin, 5 projects*, Birkhäuser, Berlim, 1994.

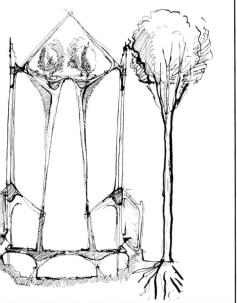

> Cathedral of St. John the Divine, New York

propuesta; los otros dos participantes presentaron soluciones radicalmente nuevas. No se consideró necesario que el jurado se reuniera nuevamente. Los proyectos se presentaron el 17 de junio, en sesión no pública; al parecer tampoco se han conservado las actas de dicha reunión. El 19 de junio se pudo leer en la prensa berlinesa que la decisión había recaído en favor de Norman Foster. El 21 de junio, la Comisión de urbanismo de la Mesa del Parlamento, sin haber solicitado informes de expertos, decidió dar el encargo al arquitecto británico. El 1 de julio, y bajo la presidencia de Rita Süssmuth, la Presidente del Bundestag, la comisión decidió solicitar de Foster no sólo que presentara planos más detallados, sino también que reconsiderara la idea de una cúpula, tal como había propuesto Calatrava.»[21] El proyecto definitivo de Foster fue aprobado por el Bundestag el 29 de junio de 1994. Santiago Calatrava hizo referencia claramente a que el proyecto final de Foster se parecía sospechosamente a su propia propuesta, lo que Foster rechazó por considerarlo infundado.

Otro interesante proyecto no construido de Santiago Calatrava fue el que ganó el concurso para la Catedral de St. John the Divine (Nueva York, 1991). Este célebre monumento de Manhattan, construido en 1892 y transformado en gótico en 1911, es la mayor iglesia neogótica del mundo. Calatrava propuso añadir elementos estructurales de apariencia orgánica, para crear una especie de «bio-refugio» a 55 metros sobre el nivel del templo. Las iglesias góticas se inspiran originalmente en la metáfora del árbol, y Calatrava partió de este hecho para añadir un jardín en el cielo, que correspondería al follaje del árbol metafórico, pero que también sería un eco del paraíso terrenal.

Este último proyecto, abundamentemente ilustrado con sus dibujos y maquetas como los demás, documenta la búsqueda de un significado más profundo en la arquitectura contemporánea por parte de Santiago Calatrava. Aquí, como en gran parte de sus proyectos de mayores dimensiones, se aprecia una investigación no sólo de soluciones funcionales, sino también de referencias plenas

progetti il 17 giugno non avvenne in forma pubblica, e pare che non ne esista documentazione alcuna. Il 19 giugno si poteva leggere sulla stampa berlinese che si era deciso in favore di Sir Norman Foster. Il 21 giugno la Commissione urbanistica del Consiglio degli anziani, senza aver chiesto il parere di un esperto, stabiliva di affidare l'incarico all'architetto inglese. Il 1° luglio, presente Rita Süssmuth, presidente del Parlamento, venne deciso di chiedere a Foster non solo di fornire disegni più dettagliati, ma anche di riconsiderare l'idea di una cupola, come proposto da Calatrava».[21] Il progetto di Foster, con le nuove modifiche, è stato approvato dal Bundestag il 29 giugno 1994. Santiago Calatrava ha chiaramente espresso l'opinione che il progetto finale dell'architetto inglese somigliava moltissimo alla propria concezione originale, un'accusa che Foster ha liquidato come infondata.

Un altro interessante progetto di Calatrava rimasto sulla carta è quello che ha vinto il concorso per la cattedrale di St. John the Divine (New York, 1991). Costruito nel 1892 e «goticizzato» nel 1911, questo famoso monumento di Manhattan è la più vasta chiesa neogotica del mondo. Aggiungendo elementi strutturali dall'aspetto organico, Calatrava propose di creare una specie di «bio-rifugio» posto a un'altezza di 55 m rispetto al pavimento dell'edificio sacro. La concezione delle chiese gotiche s'ispirava in origine alla metafora dell'albero, e Calatrava è partito da questo assunto per inserire un giardino pensile, che poteva corrispondere al fogliame dell'albero metaforico ma che allo stesso tempo si riconnetteva all'Eden.

Anch'esso copiosamente illustrato da disegni e modelli, il progetto per St. John the Divine sottolinea la ricerca dell'architetto di significati più profondi nell'architettura contemporanea. Qui, come nella maggior parte dei suoi lavori più importanti, si legge una vera ricerca non solo di soluzioni funzionali ma anche di riferimenti densi di significato. Non sempre questi ultimi risultano evidenti, collegati come sono all'immaginazione di Calatrava o alle sue sculture, e tuttavia essi manifestano un'autenticità che spiega

de sentido. Estas no siempre resultan evidentes, pues nacen de la imaginación misma de Calatrava o de sus esculturas, y sin embargo manifiestan tal autenticidad que en poco tiempo se ha convertido en uno de los arquitectos-ingenieros más famosos del mundo. Uno de los términos preferidos por Santiago Calatrava es el de «transgresión», concepto de definición propia que implica un estudio cuidadoso y conocimientos prácticos aplicados al deseo de crear formas sorprendentes. En sus manos, los puentes y las estaciones cobran nueva vida y abandonan el seco funcionalismo que les caracterizó durante el periodo de reconstrucción de la posguerra. Desarrollándose a partir de sus bocetos y esculturas, Santiago Calatrava trabaja en un campo particularmente creativo, en el que se dan cita no sólo el arte y la arquitectura, sino también la arquitectura y la ingeniería. Las palabras que Davioud pronunció en 1877, haciendo referencia a la armonía entre el arquitecto y el ingeniero, que «no llegará nunca a ser real, completa y fructífera hasta el día en que el ingeniero, el artista y el hombre de ciencia estén fundidos en una misma persona», posiblemente sean las que mejor retraten a Santiago Calatrava.

come egli sia rapidamente diventato uno degli architetti-ingegneri più famosi del mondo. «Trasgressione», uno dei suoi termini preferiti, viene da lui definita come studio attento e conoscenza pratica approfondita, messi al servizio del desiderio di creare forme sorprendenti. Nelle sue mani, ponti e stazioni ferroviarie hanno iniziato a rivivere, lasciandosi alle spalle l'arido funzionalismo affermatosi durante la ricostruzione postbellica. Procedendo a partire da disegni e sculture da lui creati, Santiago Calatrava lavora in un campo molto particolare, dove l'arte e l'architettura, e l'architettura e l'ingegneria, s'incontrano. Le parole pronunciate da Davioud nel 1877 sull'accordo tra architettura e ingegneria, che, a suo parere, non sarà mai «vero, completo e fruttuoso fino a quando l'ingegnere, l'artista e lo scienziato non si fonderanno in una stessa persona», potrebbero efficacemente descrivere un talento come quello di Santiago Calatrava.

1 Entrevista con Santiago Calatrava, París, noviembre de 1995.
2 Giedion, Sigfried: *Space, Time and Architecture*, Harvard University Press, Cambridge, Massachusetts, 51976. Edición en castellano: Espacio, Tiempo y Arquitectura, Dossat, Madrid 51979.
3 McQuaid, Matilda: *Santiago Calatrava, Structure and Expression*; The Museum of Modern Art, Nueva York 1993.
4 Ibid.
5 Entrevista con Santiago Calatrava, Zúrich, junio de 1997.
6 Ibid.
7 Nervi, Pier Luigi: *Aesthetics and Technology in Building, The Charles Eliot Norton Lectures*, 1961–1962, Harvard University Press, Cambridge, Massachusetts, 1965.
8 Entrevista con Santiago Calatrava, Zúrich, junio de 1997.
9 Ibid.
10 Ibid.
11 Ibid.
12 Ibid.
13 Ibid.
14 Sharp, Dennis (ed.): *Santiago Calatrava*, Architectural Monographs n°. 46, Academy Editions, Londres 1996.
15 Ibid.
16 Entrevista con Santiago Calatrava, Zúrich, junio de 1997.
17 Ibid.
18 Polano, Sergio: *Santiago Calatrava, Complete Works*; Gingko, Electa, Milán 1996. Edición en castellano: Santiago Calatrava, Obra Completa; Electa, Madrid 1996.
19 *Santiago Calatrava*, 1983-93: Catálogo de la exposición antológica en la Lonja de Valencia del 31 de mayo al 30 de junio de 1993, El Croquis Editorial, Madrid 1993.
20 Polano, Sergio: *Santiago Calatrava, Complete Works*; Gingko, Electa, Milán 1996. Edición en castellano: Santiago Calatrava, Obra Completa; Electa, Madrid 1996.
21 Cullen, Michael: *Calatrava Berlin, 5 projects*, Birkhäuser, Berlín 1994.

1 Intervista a Santiago Calatrava, Parigi, novembre 1995.
2 Giedion, Sigfried, *Space, Time and Architecture*, Harvard University Press, Cambridge, MA, 1976[5] [trad. it. *Spazio, tempo e architettura*, Milano, 1954].
3 McQuaid, Matilda, *Santiago Calatrava, Structure and Expression*, The Museum of Modern Art, New York, 1993.
4 *Ibid.*
5 Intervista a Santiago Calatrava, Zurigo, giugno 1997.
6 *Ibid.*
7 Nervi, Pier Luigi, *Aesthetics and Technology in Building. The Charles Eliot Norton Lectures*, 1961–1962, Harvard University Press, Cambridge, MA, 1965.
8 Intervista a Santiago Calatrava, Zurigo, giugno 1997.
9 *Ibid.*
10 *Ibid.*
11 *Ibid.*
12 *Ibid.*
13 *Ibid.*
14 Sharp Dennis (a cura di), *Santiago Calatrava*, Architectural Monographs n. 6, Academy Editions, Londra, 1996.
15 *Ibid.*
16 Intervista a Santiago Calatrava, Zurigo, giugno 1997.
17 *Ibid.*
18 Polano, Sergio, *Santiago Calatrava, Complete Works*, Gingko, Electa, Milano, 1996 [trad. it. *Santiago Calatrava. Opera completa*, Electa, Milano, 1996].
19 *Santiago Calatrava, 1983–93*, Catalogo de la exposición antológica en la Lonja de Valencia del 31 de Mayo al 30 de Junio de 1993, El Croquis Editorial, Madrid, 1993.
20 Polano, *op.cit.*
21 Cullen, Michael, *Calatrava Berlin, 5 projects*, Birkhäuser, Berlino, 1994.

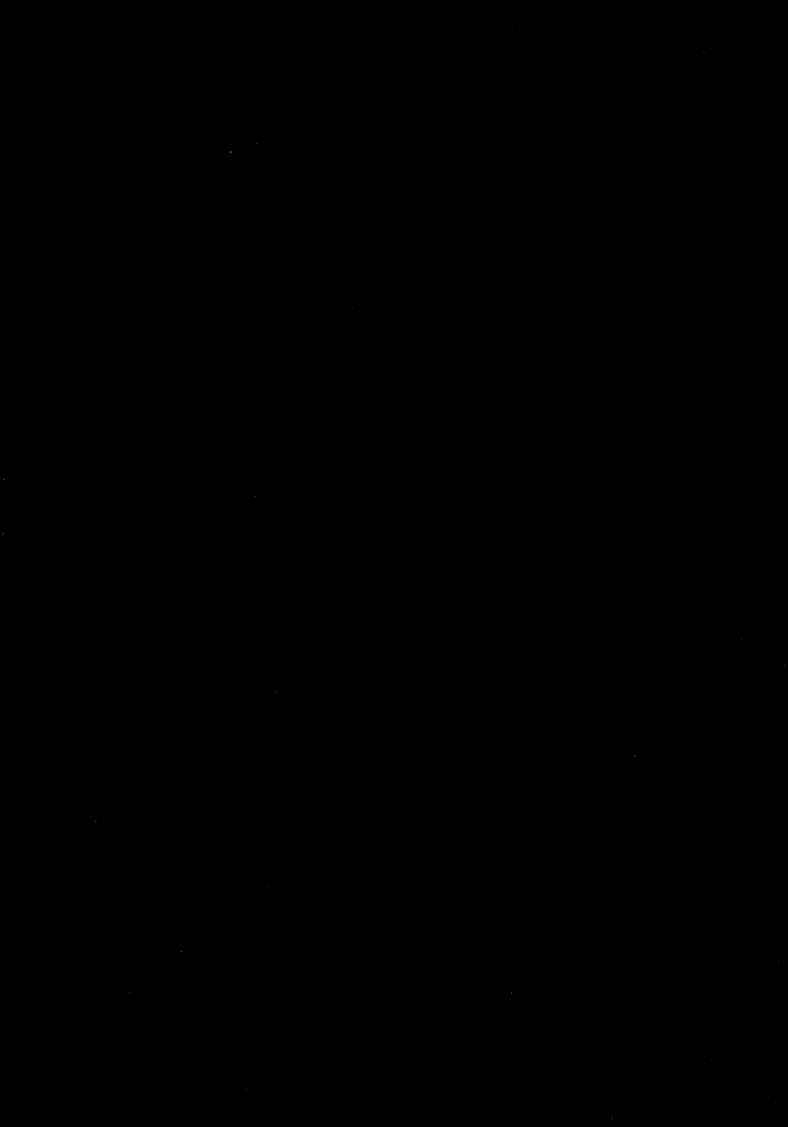

Proyectos > Progetti > Projectos

El proyecto de Santiago Calatrava para el nuevo aeropuerto de Bilbao-Sondica incluía la construcción de una Torre de Control de 42 metros de altura, situada a unos 270 metros de la nueva terminal. Invirtiendo la tipología usual en este tipo de construcciones, la torre aumenta de volumen según crece, culminando en la sala de control que ofrece una vista panorámica de 360 grados. Construida en hormigón armado con un revestimiento de aluminio, esta torre es el edificio emblemático del aeropuerto, que dispone de una terminal de 29.000 metros cuadrados distribuidos en cuatro niveles. Este edificio, que en el alzado recuerda un párpado y en la planta una manta raya con espinas de acero, puede gestionar simultáneamente la llegada y la salida de ocho aviones, gracias a sus dos alas laterales, que también permiten una posterior ampliación. Este proyecto subraya la voluntad de Bilbao de competir, desde el punto de vista arquitectónico y cultural, con ciudades del sur de España como Sevilla.

Os planos de Calatrava para as novas instalações do aeroporto de Bilbau compreendiam a construção de uma torre de controlo com 42 m de altura, implantada a cerca de 270 m do edifício do terminal. Constituindo uma inversão da tipologia normal deste género de estruturas, a torre adquire volume à medida que se eleva, culminando numa sala de controlo com uma vista panorâmica de 360°. Construída em betão armado e parcialmente coberta de alumínio, é o símbolo do próprio aeroporto, com o seu terminal de 29 000 m^2 distribuídos por quatro níveis. Assemelhando-se a uma pálpebra em elevação, ou mesmo, em plano, a uma raia com arestas de aço, a estrutura pode suportar em simultâneo a chegada e a partida de oito aviões, graças às alas laterais, as quais foram concebidas a pensar numa futura extensão. Uma vez mais, este projecto sublinha a vontade de Bilbau de concorrer em termos de arquitectura e cultura com as cidades do sul de Espanha como Sevilha.

Il progetto di Santiago Calatrava per le nuove installazioni dell'aeroporto di Sondica comprendeva la costruzione di una torre di controllo alta 42 m, situata a circa 270 m dall'edificio del terminal. Sovvertendo la normale tipologia di questo genere di strutture, la torre acquista progressivamente volume in rapporto all'altezza, culminando in una sala di controllo da cui si apre una veduta a 360 gradi. Costruita in cemento armato con parziale rivestimento in alluminio, la torre è un simbolo dell'aeroporto stesso, il quale dispone di un'area servizi di 29.000 m^2 suddivisa su quattro livelli. La torre – il cui alzato riecheggia la forma di una palpebra, e la pianta forse una manta dalle spine d'acciaio – è in grado di gestire simultaneamente l'arrivo e la partenza di otto aerei, grazie ad ali laterali predisposte per una futura espansione. Questo progetto rispecchia la volontà di Bilbao di competere, sotto i punti di vista architettonico e culturale, con città del Sud della Spagna come Siviglia.

Sondica Airport and Control Tower,
Bilbao, Spain, 1990–2000

El elemento más espectacular de este proyecto es el puente de la Alameda, que atraviesa el lecho seco del Turia. Como otros puentes diseñados por Calatrava, se caracteriza por un arco parabólico de acero pintado, inclinado con un ángulo de 30 grados, que mide 14 metros desde el firme hasta la cúspide. La calzada del puente, de 26 metros de anchura y 130 metros de largo, se extiende justo por encima y en paralelo a la Estación de Metro, también obra de Calatrava. Construcciones en forma de boca dan acceso a los andenes del metro, de 63 metros de longitud, que recuerdan la tesis titulada «Sobre la plegabilidad de las cerchas», con la que Calatrava se doctoró en el año 1981 en la Universidad Técnica Helvética (ETH) de Zúrich. Las taquillas se encuentran situadas en cada extremo de los andenes. Al nivel del lecho del río, una cubierta reticular de vidrio translúcido proporciona luz cenital al interior de la estación, mientras que por la noche permite reconocer la plaza exterior. El uso de azulejerías fragmentadas para coronar las superficies de los muros recuerda la tradición de Gaudí.

O aspecto mais espectacular deste projecto é, muito naturalmente, a ponte da Alameda que atravessa o leito seco do rio Turia. Como outras obras de arte de Calatrava, esta emprega um arco parabólico em aço pintado, inclinado a 30°, elevando-se até atingir os 14 m acima da superfície do amplo tabuleiro. Este último, com 26 m de largura e 130 m de abertura, encontra-se paralelamente sobre a estação do metropolitano, também esta uma obra do arquitecto. As estruturas em forma de boca, as quais dão acesso às plataformas do metropolitano, estendendo-se estas por 63 m, relembram a tese de doutoramento de Calatrava concernente ao «Encurvamento de Estruturas Tridimensionais». Os postigos de venda de bilhetes estão situados nas duas extremidades das plataformas. Ao nível do leito do rio, existe um tecto estriado com lanternins de vidro translúcido, permitindo a entrada de luz natural para o interior da estação e a iluminação exterior da praça durante a noite. O acabamento das paredes em azulejo partido evoca indirectamente a tradição de Gaudí.

L'aspetto più spettacolare di questo progetto è naturalmente il ponte di Alameda, che attraversa il letto asciutto del fiume Turia. Come molti altri ponti disegnati da Calatrava, anche questo si avvale di un arco parabolico in acciaio dipinto, con un'inclinazione di 30 gradi, che s'innalza a un'altezza massima di 14 m sopra il piano stradale. Largo 26 m, il ponte ha una luce di 130 m e corre parallelamente al di sopra della stazione della metropolitana, anch'essa progettata da Calatrava. I moduli ribaltabili a forma di bocca dei portali di accesso ai binari sotterranei, lunghi 63 m, ricordano che la tesi di dottorato presentata nel 1981 da Calatrava all'ETH di Zurigo riguardava la piegabilità delle strutture. Alle due estremità dei binari sono situati gli sportelli per la vendita dei biglietti. Una copertura nervata a livello del letto del fiume, con aperture vetrate, lascia penetrare la luce del giorno all'interno della stazione e segnala di notte la presenza del piazzale esterno. Il rivestimento a mosaico dei muri richiama indirettamente la tradizione di Gaudí.

Alameda Bridge and Underground Station,
Valencia, Spain, 1991–95

Este puente fue encargado por la Junta de Andalucía con ocasión de la Expo 92. Se extiende, con uná luz de 200 metros, sobre el meandro de San Jerónimo, un afluente del Guadalquivir. El elemento más espectacular es un mástil de 142 metros de altura, con una inclinación de 58 grados —idéntica a la de la gran pirámide de Keops—. Macizado de hormigón, su peso es suficiente para servir de contrapeso al tablero, con lo que los tensores resultan superfluos. El planteamiento personal de Calatrava recuerda una escultura que hizo él mismo en 1986, denominada «Torso en movimiento», en la que varios cubos de mármol situados uno sobre otro se mantienen en equilibrio gracias a un cable tensado. Originalmente, propuso un segundo puente con un mástil idéntico, inclinado en el sentido opuesto, pero el cliente prefirió el Viaducto de La Cartuja, de 500 metros de longitud, que servía de entrada norte a la Expo 92. Imitado ya por otros arquitectos e ingenieros, el mástil inclinado del Puente del Alamillo se ha convertido en un símbolo de la Sevilla moderna.

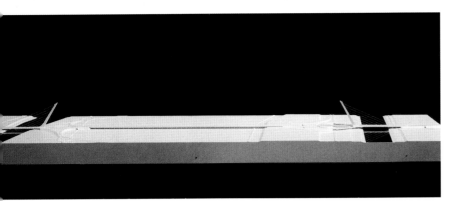

Esta ponte, com 200 m de abertura, que atravessa o Meandro San Jeronimo, um afluente do Guadalquivir, foi construída no âmbito do plano de urbanização lançado pelo governo da Região de Andaluzia aquando da Expo '92. A sua característica mais impressionante é o pilão de 142 m de altura, inclinado sobre um ângulo de 58°, idêntico ao da pirâmide de Keops. O peso desta estrutura repleta de betão é suficiente para contrabalançar o do tabuleiro, eliminando a necessidade de cabos traseiros. A aproximação bastante pessoal escolhida por Calatrava aponta para uma das suas esculturas, «Torso corredor» (1986), elaborada com cubos de mármore equilibrados por um fio tensor de ferro, bem como para os seus desenhos de figuras em pleno movimento. Originalmente, Calatrava propusera uma segunda ponte sustentada por um pilão similar, mas inclinado no sentido oposto; porém, foi preterida em favor do viaduto com 500 m de La Cartuja, o qual servia de entrada norte ao local da Expo. Várias vezes reproduzido por outros engenheiros e arquitectos, o pilão da ponte do Alamillo tornou-se um dos símbolos da modernidade sevilhana.

Questo ponte, commissionato dalla Junta dell'Andalusia in occasione dell'Expo '92, ha una luce di 200 m e supera il Meandro San Jeronimo, un ramo del Guadalquivir. Il suo elemento più impressionante è un pilone alto 142 m, inclinato di 58 gradi, proprio come la piramide di Cheope. La massa di questa struttura, riempita di calcestruzzo, è sufficiente a controbilanciare il peso dell'impalcato, eliminando la necessità di stralli posteriori. L'originale soluzione proposta da Calatrava per il ponte di Alamillo si ricollega a una sua scultura del 1986, intitolata *Torso in corsa*, costituita da una pila inclinata di cubi di marmo tenuta in equilibrio da un filo metallico in tensione, ma anche ai suoi disegni di figure in movimento. In origine Calatrava aveva proposto un secondo ponte inclinato nella direzione opposta, immagine speculare del primo, ma il committente optò per il viadotto del Puente de la Cartuja, lungo 500 m, che venne utilizzato come ingresso nord all'area dell'Expo '92. Frequentemente imitato da altri ingegneri e architetti, il pilone inclinato del ponte di Alamillo è diventato un simbolo della Siviglia moderna.

Alamillo Bridge and La Cartuja Viaduct,
Seville, Spain, 1987–92

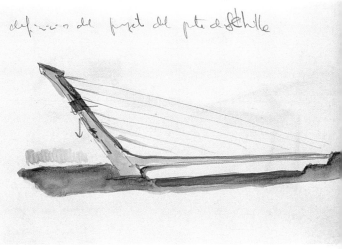

Alamillo Bridge and La Cartuja Viaduct, Seville, Spain   58 ◄ 59

La tipología estructural del árbol, latente en proyectos tan diversos como la Estación de Oriente de Lisboa, el Museo de Ciencias de Valencia y el proyecto para la Catedral de St. John the Divine de Nueva York, se puede apreciar igualmente en Bell Canada Enterprises Place, Gallery & Heritage Square de Toronto. Calatrava colaboró con el estudio neoyorquino de los arquitectos Skidmore, Owings & Merrill para crear una galería de seis plantas y 115 metros de longitud que conecta dos torres mediante un pasadizo de cristal y acero pintado de blanco. Como comentó el New York Times, «Esta galería parece hecha por Gaudí.» Como en el caso de la Catedral de Nueva York, aquí Calatrava también se remonta a la raíces de la arquitectura occidental, en un sentido casi literal, empleando la imagen del árbol para crear un gran espacio urbano vinculado tanto a la tradición gótica como a arquitectos más modernos, como Gaudí.

A tipologia estrutural da árvore, presente em projectos tão diferentes quanto a Estação do Oriente, em Lisboa, o Museu das Ciências de Valência e a proposta para a St. John the Divine, encontra-se igualmente patente no complexo da Bell Canada Enterprises Place, Gallery & Heritage Square, em Toronto. Aqui, Calatrava colaborou com a agência de arquitectos nova-iorquina Skidmore, Owings & Merrill para criar essa galeria com 115 m de comprimento e uma altura de seis andares, ligando duas torres através de uma passagem em aço, pintado de branco, e vidro. Como assinalou o *New York Times*, «Esta galeria vai beber a sua inspiração a Gaudí». Tomando o exemplo da catedral de Nova Iorque, Calatrava regressa às raízes da arquitectura ocidental, numa acepção quase literal, servindo-se da imagem da árvore para conceber um vasto espaço urbano, próximo tanto da tradição gótica como da de criadores mais recentes como Gaudí.

La tipologia strutturale dell'albero, presente in progetti così diversi come la stazione Oriente a Lisbona, il Museo della Scienza a Valencia e la proposta per la cattedrale di St. John the Divine, ritorna anche nel complesso del Bell Canada Enterprise Place, Gallery & Heritage Square di Toronto. Per questo progetto Calatrava ha lavorato in collaborazione con l'agenzia newyorchese dello studio di architetti Skidmore, Owings & Merrill. La realizzazione consiste in una galleria lunga 115 m e alta sei piani, la quale mette in comunicazione due torri attraverso un passaggio in acciaio dipinto di bianco e vetro. «Questa galleria è decisamente ispirata a Gaudí», ha commentato il «New York Times». Come nel caso della cattedrale di New York, con questo progetto Calatrava ritorna, quasi alla lettera, alle radici dell'architettura occidentale, utilizzando l'immagine dell'albero per creare un grande spazio urbano che si ricollega tanto alla tradizione gotica quanto all'apporto di figure più moderne quali Gaudí.

BCE Place, Gallery & Heritage Square,
Toronto, Canada, 1987–92

BCE Place, Gallery & Heritage Square, Toronto, Canada   62 ◄ 63

Este importante conjunto de estructuras construido por la Generalitat Valenciana comenzó a proyectarse hace más de una década en Valencia, la ciudad natal de Calatrava, en un terreno situado junto al viejo cauce del río Turia, a mitad de camino entre el centro de la ciudad y el barrio costero de Nazaret. Estas formas espectaculares han tomado muchos elementos propios de su lenguaje arquitectónico, como sucede con su fascinación por el globo ocular, que aquí dictó la forma del planetario de 7.100 m². Situado en un estanque plano, la estructura incluye un gran mirador volado en forma de «párpado», que alberga L'Hemisféric, un cine-planetario IMAX. El museo de 41.530 m², con su atrio largo y vertebrado, recuerda el diseño de Calatrava para BCE Place de Toronto, con su fachada vidriada y altos nervios que sustentan la estructura. El último elemento de esta composición es el Palacio de las Artes, de 44.150 m², previsto para las artes escénicas musicales, con tres auditorios: una sala principal con capacidad para 1.300 personas; una sala para música de cámara, con aforo de 400 plazas, y finalmente, un auditorio al aire libre para 2.000 personas.

Este grupo significativo de edifícios construídos para o Governo de Valência começou a tomar forma há mais de uma década na cidade natal de Calatrava, Valência, num grande local perto de Turia, a meio caminho entre a parte velha da cidade e a zona costeira de Nazaret. Muitas características típicas do seu vocabulário arquitectónico tomam aqui formas espectaculares – tal como é o caso do seu fascínio pela forma do globo ocular – que aqui ditam o *design* do Planetário com 7100 m². Situado numa bacia pouco profunda, a estrutura inclui um baldaquino em forma de pálpebra que se move e um cinema IMAX hemisférico. O museu com 41 530 m² e um átrio comprido e com vigas lembra-nos o *design* do BCE, com os seus amplos arcos envidraçados e altos. O último elemento significativo da sua obra, além da torre originalmente lisa, é o Palacio de las Artes com 44 150 m², concebido para actuações musicais na sua sala principal com 1300 lugares, no pequeno auditório com 400 lugares e no recinto aberto em forma de concha com 2000 lugares.

Il significativo gruppo di progetti realizzati per la Comunità di Valencia, città natale di Calatrava, ha preso corpo nell'arco di oltre un decennio in un ampio sito presso il fiume Turia, a metà strada tra la città vecchia e il quartiere di Nazaret posto sulla costa. Molti tratti familiari del vocabolario architettonico di Calatrava si trasformano qui in forme spettacolari, come nel caso della sua predilezione per la forma del bulbo oculare che in questo lavoro determina il disegno del Planetario di 7100 m² di superficie. Collocata in un bacino poco profondo, la struttura comprende una tettoia mobile, la «palpebra», e una sala cinematografica IMAX a cupola emisferica. Il museo, che si estende su un'area di 41.530 m², con il suo atrio d'ingresso lungo e costolonato ricorda il BCE Place, dalle alte e ampie arcate a vetri. L'ultimo elemento significativo del complesso, se si esclude la torre originariamente prevista, è il Palacio de las Artes di 44.150 m², costruito per ospitare eventi musicali in una sala principale con 1300 posti a sedere, un piccolo auditorium di 400 posti e un teatro all'aperto che può accogliere fino a 2000 spettatori.

Ciudad de las Artes y de las Ciencias, Valencia, Spain
Planetarium 1991–1998
Museum 1991–2000
Palacio de las Artes 1995–

A pesar de que no se llegó a realizar, este proyecto de Santiago Calatrava es uno de los más inspirados y simbólicos: la ampliación de una de las iglesias más conocidas de Nueva York, construida en 1892 por Heins & La Farge —en un estilo neorrománico— y transformada en gótico en 1911 por Cram & Ferguson. El proyecto de Calatrava proponía añadir un nuevo transepto orientado al sur y un «bio-refugio». Esta terraza, claramente inspirada en el paraíso terrenal, se situaría a 55 metros sobre el nivel del templo, sobre elementos arborescentes. Reemplazando el techo de la nave, este jardín no habría cambiado la silueta de la iglesia, pero habría introducido luz natural. Calatrava consiguió el primer premio del concurso; tanto el jurado como la opinión pública lo acogieron con entusiasmo, pero los recortes presupuestarios impidieron llevar el proyecto a la práctica. Como ha hecho observar Philip Johnson, por sus relaciones con el gótico original, este proyecto habría reconciliado el pasado con el futuro.

Apesar de não realizado, este projecto de Calatrava continua a ser um dos mais inspirados e simbólicos da sua carreira. Pretendendo transformar uma das igrejas nova-iorquinas mais célebres, construída originalmente em estilo neo-romano por Heins & La Farge em 1892 e «goticizada» por Cram & Ferguson em 1911, este trabalho teria permitido anexar um novo transepto a sul e um «bio-refúgio». Este último, que evoca simbolicamente o Éden original, teria sido implantado a 55 m do solo, assentando sobre elementos de inspiração arbórea. Localizado na cave da nave existente e sem modificar o perfil do edifício, o jardim teria permitido uma maior entrada de luz natural para o interior da catedral. Tal projecto, que arrebatou o primeiro prémio, foi recebido com entusiasmo pelo júri e pelo público, mas não pôde ser realizado por falta de verbas. Respeitando a decoração gótica primitiva, como sublinhou Philip Johnson, o plano conciliava o passado e o futuro.

Anche se rimasto solo sulla carta, questo progetto di Santiago Calatrava è una delle concezioni più ispirate e simboliche della sua carriera. Esso prevedeva un intervento su una delle chiese newyorchesi più famose – costruita all'origine in stile neoromanico da Heins & La Farge nel 1892 e «goticizzata» da Cram & Ferguson nel 1911 – che avrebbe comportato l'aggiunta di un nuovo transetto sud e di un «bio-rifugio». Quest'ultimo, simbolicamente collegato all'Eden delle origini, sarebbe stato una sorta di giardino pensile a 55 m da terra, sorretto da elementi strutturali ispirati alla forma dell'albero. Occupando lo spazio del sottotetto della navata, il bio-rifugio non avrebbe cambiato il profilo dell'edificio e avrebbe avuto il vantaggio di provvedere all'illuminazione naturale della cattedrale. Vincitore del primo premio al concorso, accolto entusiasticamente sia dalla giuria che dal pubblico, questo progetto non ha potuto essere realizzato per mancanza di fondi. In armonia con la decorazione gotica originale, come ha evidenziato Philip Johnson, questo lavoro riconciliava passato e futuro.

Cathedral of St. John the Divine,
New York, USA, 1991

Este auditorio, aún en construcción, se encuentra situado en la intersección de la Avenida del Tres de Mayo y la Avenida Marítima, en Santa Cruz de Tenerife. Con su cubierta de hormigón, de forma triangular curvada muy característica, que se eleva 58 metros sobre el nivel de la plaza que rodea al edificio, promete convertirse en una de las obras más espectaculares de Calatrava. Una vez más, e independientemente de las funciones que ha de cumplir el edificio, su misma apariencia le confiere valor simbólico. Ubicado en un terreno rectangular de 154 por 100 metros, con la particularidad de tener que salvar un desnivel de 60 metros, el Auditorio se levanta sobre una plataforma escalonada, una especie de plinto, que contiene las instalaciones técnicas y los camerinos. La cubierta de hormigón armado en forma de concha está revestida de azulejos fragmentados que forman un mosaico, mientras que gran parte del pavimento es de piedra volcánica de la zona. La cúpula de 50 metros de altura que corona el Auditorio remite a los estudios de Santiago Calatrava sobre el ojo y el párpado humanos.

Actualmente em construção, esta sala de concertos, com capacidade para 2000 lugares sentados, situa-se no cruzamento da avenida do Tres de Mayo um a avenida Marítima, em Santa Cruz de Tenerife. Com o seu tecto vertiginoso em betão, possuidor de uma forma triangular que culmina a 58 m acima do nível da praça que cerca o edifício, a sala deverá ser uma das estruturas mais visualmente surpreendentes erigidas até hoje pelo arquitecto. Para além das funções básicas do projecto, este cativará mais uma vez um valor simbólico através da própria natureza da sua aparência. Situada num terreno rectangular com 154 por 100 m, marcado por um desnivelamento de 60 m, a sala está edificada sobre uma plataforma em escada ou plinto, a qual contém as instalações técnicas e os camarins dos artistas. O tecto da estrutura está revestido com telha partida, e a maior parte do pavimento é feito de pedra vulcânica local. Uma cúpula com 50 m de altura cobre o auditório principal, denotando alguns estudos de Santiago Calatrava sobre o olho e a pálpebra.

Attualmente in fase di costruzione, questa sala da concerti con una capienza di 2000 posti è situata nella città di Santa Cruz de Tenerife, all'incrocio fra l'Avenida Tres de Mayo e l'Avenida Maritima. La sua suggestiva copertura curva in calcestruzzo, la cui sagoma triangolare raggiunge i 58 m di altezza massima e torreggia sul piazzale circostante, promette di farne una delle strutture più spettacolari finora concepite da Calatrava. Ancora una volta, al di là delle sue funzioni di base, l'edificio assumerà un valore simbolico grazie alla natura stessa del suo aspetto. La sala da concerti, collocata su un sito rettangolare di 154 x 100 m contrassegnato da un dislivello di 60 m, sorge su una piattaforma a gradoni o plinto, al cui interno trovano sistemazione le installazioni tecniche e i camerini per gli artisti. Il tetto della conchiglia di calcestruzzo è rivestito di piastrelle a mosaico, mentre per gran parte dei pavimenti si è fatto ricorso alla pietra vulcanica locale. La cupola alta 50 m che fa da coronamento alla sala principale richiama gli studi di Calatrava sull'occhio umano.

Tenerife Concert Hall,
Santa Cruz de Tenerife, Canary Islands, Spain, 1991–

Tenerife Concert Hall, Santa Cruz de Tenerife, Canary Islands, Spain

Construido por las autoridades municipales de Tenerife, no lejos del centro de la ciudad, este proyecto forma parte del programa de reordenación del paseo marítimo de Santa Cruz, donde antiguamente se encontraban una escombrera y una refinería de petróleo. Un arco rebajado —de 39 metros de altura en el punto máximo— cubre un pabellón multiuso de 270 metros de longitud con un aforo de unas 3000 personas. Como en la mayoría de los proyectos de Calatrava, se emplean distintos materiales dependiendo de la altura del edificio. El hormigón oscurecido con grava volcánica deja paso al acero en el arco principal. El flexible diseño del Centro de Exposiciones permite organizar acontecimientos de pequeña escala o también ferias, conciertos y el carnaval de Tenerife, que se celebrará aquí anualmente.

Construído por encomenda do governo de Tenerife, perto do centro antigo da cidade, este projecto está incluído no programa de recuperação da zona marítima de Santa Cruz, antiga localização de uma lixeira e de uma refinaria de petróleo. Em 1991, logo que Calatrava foi declarado vencedor do concurso para este projecto, propôs, como geralmente faz, transformá-lo numa operação de renovação urbana. Um arco baixo, com uma abertura de 270 m, cobre um átrio polivalente com capacidade para cerca de 3000 pessoas, atingindo a altura máxima interior de 39 m. Como muitas vezes acontece com Calatrava, os materiais mudam à medida que a construção avança. Neste caso, para a formação do arco principal, o betão, escurecido pela mistura de saibro vulcânico local, deu lugar ao aço. A concepção flexível deste centro permite a organização de pequenas manifestações, feiras, concertos e ainda estabelecer aqui o Carnaval de Tenerife, que ocorrerá todos os anos.

Costruito per la municipalità di Tenerife, nei pressi della città vecchia, quest'opera è inclusa nel programma di ripristino di una zona del lungomare di Santa Cruz, già sede di una discarica e di una raffineria. Quando nel 1991 Calatrava ha vinto il concorso bandito per questo progetto, si è ritrovato, come spesso gli accade, a difendere in modo convincente la causa del rinnovamento urbano. Un arco ribassato scavalca una sala polivalente lunga 270 m e con un'altezza massima interna di 39 m, in grado di contenere circa 3000 persone. Come in molti lavori di Calatrava, i materiali cambiano via via che la struttura si eleva nello spazio. Qui il calcestruzzo, reso più scuro dall'aggiunta di ghiaia vulcanica locale, cede il passo all'acciaio nella realizzazione del grande arco. Il design flessibile del centro d'esposizioni permette l'organizzazione di piccole manifestazioni come di grandi fiere e concerti, e anche del Carnevale di Tenerife, che si terrà qui annualmente.

Tenerife Exhibition Center,
Santa Cruz de Tenerife, Canary Islands, Spain, 1992–95

En el contexto de la construcción de una línea de alta velocidad entre Lieja y Bruselas, que se concluirá en el 2002, y que probablemente se continúe hasta la frontera alemana en el 2005, Santiago Calatrava ganó, imponiéndose a Nicholas Grimshaw y Aldo Rossi, el concurso para construir la nueva estación. Como dijo en el momento de anunciar el resultado Michel Daerden, ministro belga de transporte, su experiencia con una estación similar como la de Stadelhofen en Zúrich, fue decisiva para que el jurado se inclinara por Calatrava. Tanto la estación de Zúrich como la de Lieja se encuentran sobre un terreno accidentado; y en un caso como en el otro se ha previsto que el tráfico ferroviario no se interrumpa durante las obras de construcción. Según Santiago Calatrava, una de las peculiaridades esenciales de la nueva estación es la ausencia de una fachada claramente definida. Su lugar lo ocuparán una plaza abierta y un acceso sin barreras para subrayar sus principios de permeabilidad y comunicación.

É no quadro da construção de uma ligação ferroviária a grande velocidade entre Liège e Bruxelas, a qual deverá estar completa em 2002 e eventualmente alargada até à Alemanha em 2005, que Santiago Calatrava foi seleccionado durante o concurso para esta nova estação, afastando Nicholas Grimshaw e Aldo Rossi. Michel Daerden, ministro dos transportes belga, declarou que a experiência similar do arquitecto com a estação de Stadelhofen em Zurique orientou claramente a escolha do júri. Também aqui, as instalações situam-se na encosta de uma colina, e o tráfego ferroviário não deverá ser interrompido durante a sua edificação. Segundo o arquitecto, uma das características essenciais desta estação consistirá na ausência de uma fachada identificável. Tratar-se-á antes de um espaço aberto de livre acesso, ilustrando, aliás, os seus princípios de permeabilidade e comunicação, dos quais não prescinde.

Questa nuova struttura della città belga viene realizzata nell'ambito della costruzione di una linea ferroviaria ad alta velocità destinata, entro il 2002, a collegare Liegi a Bruxelles, e successivamente (2005) a prolungarsi verso la Germania. Con il suo progetto Calatrava ha vinto un concorso fra i cui partecipanti figuravano Nicholas Grimshaw e Aldo Rossi. Senza dubbio, come ha affermato il ministro dei Trasporti belga Michel Daerden annunciando l'incarico dell'architetto spagnolo, la sua esperienza con l'analoga stazione di Stadelhofen a Zurigo ha avuto un peso essenziale nell'orientare la giuria in questa scelta. A Liegi, come a Zurigo, l'installazione è situata su una collina e continua a rimanere operativa anche durante la fase di costruzione. L'architetto ha affermato che uno dei tratti distintivi della nuova stazione sarà l'assenza di una facciata che la definisca. Un piazzale aperto e un accesso privo di barriere saranno gli elementi che illustreranno i suoi principi, sempre coerenti, di permeabilità e di comunicazione.

Liège Railway Station,
Liège, Belgium, 1996–

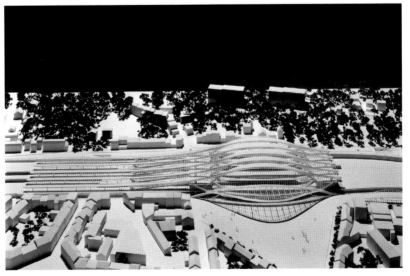

Liège Railway Station, Liège, Belgium

Construido como parte de la actividades de reordenación de la estación de Lucerna, este pórtico se divide en tres niveles. Entre un área comercial en la planta inferior y un restaurante en la superior, el espacio principal sirve de mediación entre la auténtica fachada de la estación y el centro de la ciudad de Lucerna. El pórtico mide 109 metros de longitud y 14 de anchura. Una espectacular construcción suspendida a 19 metros de altura descansa sobre 16 pilares inclinados «antropomorfos», en forma de F, de acero y hormigón, que sobresalen en voladizo sobre la calle. La cubierta es ligera, de acero y cristal, y está sostenida por los pilares, extendiéndose entre el pórtico y la fachada de la estación mediante un sistema de tensión triangular. El vestíbulo creado bajo este techo constituye un acceso luminoso, etéreo y espacioso, que facilita el movimiento de los viajeros.

Inserido no âmbito do programa de renovação da estação de Lucerna, este átrio está distribuído por três níveis: zonas comerciais no subsolo, um restaurante logo acima, e um espaço principal que faz a ligação entre a verdadeira fachada da estação e o centro da cidade de Lucerna. O pórtico mede 109 m de comprimento por 14 m de largura. Suspenso a 19 m de altura, o tecto espectacular está apoiado sobre um conjunto de 16 colunas «antropomórficas» e inclinadas em forma de F, de betão e aço, debruçando-se para a rua. Em vidro e aço, sustentado pelas colunas, o tecto leve estende-se para além do pórtico e da fachada da estação através de um sistema tensor triangular. O átrio resultante constitui uma entrada luminosa, arejada e espaçosa que facilita o movimento dos passageiros.

Realizzato nell'ambito del programma di rinnovamento della stazione ferroviaria di Lucerna, questo atrio si sviluppa su tre livelli: una zona commerciale sotterranea, un ristorante sopraelevato e un grande spazio d'accoglienza che fa da mediatore tra la vera facciata della stazione e il centro della città di Lucerna. Il portico è lungo 109 m e largo 14. Uno spettacolare «tetto» sospeso, alto 19 m, poggia su 16 colonne «antropomorfiche» a forma di F, in calcestruzzo e acciaio, inclinate verso la strada. Il tetto vero e proprio, in acciaio leggero e vetro, si estende tra questo portico e la facciata della stazione mediante un sistema triangolare di tensione. Il nuovo spazio così ricavato diventa un atrio arioso e pieno di luce, che facilita la circolazione dei passeggeri in arrivo o in partenza.

Lucerne Station Hall,
Lucerne, Switzerland, 1983–89

Lucerne Station Hall, Lucerne, Switzerland

Santiago Calatrava describe este edificio en términos antropomorfos. «Su forma plana quiere sugerir una idea de bienvenida y hospitalidad —dice—, una invitación para reunirse y rezar. La imagen de dos manos que casi se tocan simboliza cómo la estructura asciende lentamente». Esas manos que se pueden juntar para rezar o se pueden abrir al cielo y los arcos —otro de los motivos favoritos de Calatrava— proceden del repertorio de formas del espacio interior gótico, de los proyectos más antiguos para catedrales. Aquí, como en varias de sus otras obras, el arquitecto busca un método que recuerde las más profundas fuentes del diseño arquitectónico, mientras que pone al día las imágenes y las hace así únicas. En el caso de Oakland, este proyecto pretendía «modelar la línea de rascacielos» de la ciudad, pero al mismo tiempo crear una conexión profunda con el entorno urbano. De hecho, el arquitecto habla de un «campus de la catedral», en el que la iglesia misma se convierte en el «elemento central de los diferentes edificios anexos y de los espacios exteriores que organiza ella misma». Para ello emplea la metáfora de la «Ciudad de Dios» (Civitas Dei), una idea que hunde sus raíces en la historia de la espiritualidad.

Santiago Calatrava descreve este edifício em termos antropomórficos: «A sua forma simples pretende sugerir uma ideia de boas-vindas e hospitalidade», diz ele, «um convite à reunião e devoção. A imagem de duas mãos que quase se tocam desmaterializa-se à medida que a estrutura ascende». A ideia das duas mãos em posição de oração ou de um baldaquino arborizado, outro dos motivos preferidos de Calatrava, estão, sem dúvida, entre as fontes dos mais antigos *designs* de catedrais. Aqui, como em muitas das suas obras, o arquitecto procura um método que ponha em prática as fontes intrínsecas do *design*, ao passo que actualiza as imagens tornando-as indubitavelmente únicas. No caso de Oakland, o seu projecto propõe-se a «modelar a linha do horizonte» da cidade, mas também a criar uma ligação profunda com o meio urbano envolvente. Na verdade, ele fala de um «*campus* catedral», no qual a própria igreja torna-se o «elemento nuclear a partir do qual os diferentes edifícios anexos e os espaços exteriores se organizam». Aqui, ele remete para a imagem da «cidade de Deus» (Civitas Dei), de facto uma ideia com raízes muito profundas na história da espiritualidade.

Santiago Calatrava descrive questo edificio in termini antropomorfici: «La sua semplice forma vuole suggerire un'idea di accoglienza e ospitalità,» dice l'architetto, «un invito al raccoglimento e alla devozione. L'immagine di due mani quasi unite che si smaterializzano con l'elevarsi della struttura». Le mani giunte in preghiera o la tettoia che suggerisce l'impressione di una foresta, un altro dei motivi preferiti da Calatrava, in realtà sono i temi ispiratori di molte antiche cattedrali. Qui, come del resto nella gran parte dei suoi lavori, l'architetto sperimenta un metodo che si rifà alle più profonde origini del disegno, mentre ne attualizza gli edifici rendendoli unici. Nel caso di Oakland, il suo progetto intende «modellare lo skyline» della città, ma anche creare una profonda connessione con l'ambiente urbano. Infatti, Calatrava parla di «campus della cattedrale» nel quale la chiesa stessa diviene il «fulcro attorno al quale i diversi edifici annessi e gli spazi esterni si organizzano». Qui Calatrava riprende l'immagine della Civitas Dei, la città di Dio, un concetto che affonda le proprie radici nella storia della spiritualità.

Oakland Diocese Cathedral Campus Project,
Oakland, California, USA, 2000–

Es éste uno de los proyectos más recientes de Calatrava y al mismo tiempo de uno en sus primeros encargos en Estados Unidos. La estructura cruciforme servirá de nueva entrada y zona de exposiciones temporales para el Memorial de la guerra y la Galería de Arte construidos por Eero Saarinen en 1957. Con un presupuesto de 27 millones de dólares, Calatrava propuso añadir una pasarela para unir la ciudad con este solar. El proyecto resulta acorde con sus planteamientos usuales de las zonas urbanas, pues salva una pendiente de diez metros y una autopista que separan la ciudad del museo. Situado en una orilla del Lago Michigan y alineado con una de las principales avenidas de Milwaukee, se ha comparado el pabellón con las alas abiertas de un cisne. El director del museo, Russell Bowman, ha comentado: «Buscamos un arquitecto que estuviera en condiciones de llevarnos más allá de lo que nos podíamos imaginar.»

Sendo um dos projectos mais recentes de Calatrava e uma das suas primeiras encomendas americanas, esta estrutura funcionará como nova entrada e espaço de exposições temporárias para o maciço e cruciforme monumento aos mortos da guerra e centro de exposições construído em 1957 por Eero Saarinen. Respeitando o orçamento de 27 milhões de dólares, Calatrava propôs a construção de uma passagem para peões, a qual, transpondo um declive de 10 m e uma via rápida, permite ligar a cidade ao local. Tal gesto insere-se perfeitamente no espírito de prática urbana do arquitecto. Situado na margem do Lago Michigan e alinhado com uma das avenidas principais de Milwaukee, o traçado deste pavilhão foi já comparado às asas abertas de um cisne. O director do museu, Russell Bowman, observou: «Pretendíamos um arquitecto que nos conduzisse até territórios nunca antes imaginados».

Questa struttura è uno dei più recenti progetti di Calatrava ed è anche una delle sue prime realizzazioni negli Stati Uniti. Si tratta di una nuova zona di accesso (destinata anche a ospitare esposizioni temporanee) all'imponente monumento ai Caduti e museo d'arte d'impianto cruciforme creato nel 1957 da Eero Saarinen. Con un budget di 27 milioni di dollari, Calatrava propone di aggiungere un ponte pedonale che colleghi il sito alla città, finora separati da una depressione del terreno profonda 10 m e dal passaggio di un'autostrada: un'idea che è perfettamente in sintonia con il suo abituale modo di procedere negli interventi su aree urbane. Situato in riva al lago Michigan e allineato a una delle strade principali di Milwaukee, il padiglione concepito da Calatrava presenta una forma che è stata paragonata alle ali dispiegate di un cigno. Russell Bowman, il direttore del museo, ha dichiarato: «Volevamo un architetto che ci portasse al di là di ogni nostra possibile immaginazione».

Extension for the Milwaukee Art Museum,
Milwaukee, Wisconsin, USA, 1994–2001

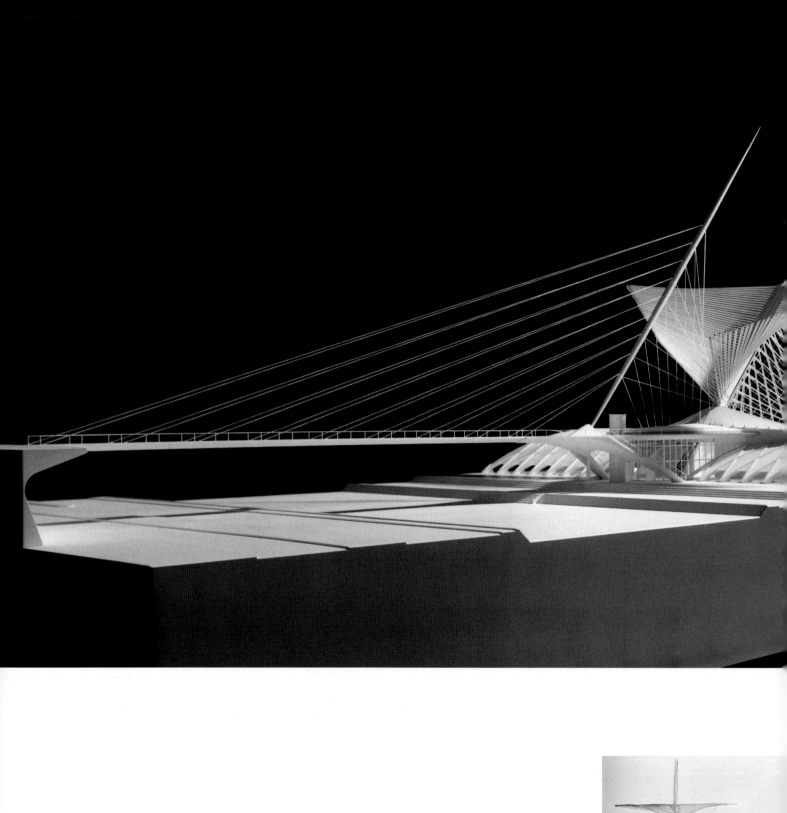

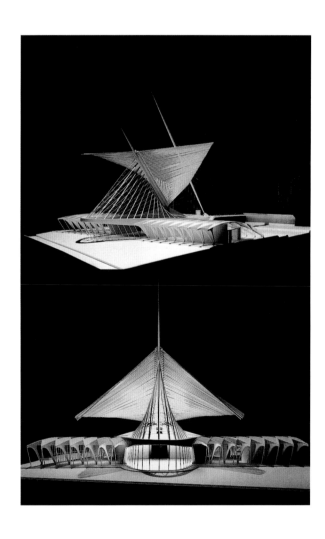

Situada cerca del Palau Sant Jordi, construido por el arquitecto japonés Arata Isozaki, la Torre de Comunicaciones de Montjuic alcanza los 130 metros de altura. Se construyó con ocasión de los Juegos Olímpicos celebrados en la ciudad condal y consta de un fuste inclinado sobre una base semicircular. Aunque recuerda una jabalina, se inspira en dibujos de Calatrava que representan una figura humana arrodillada para hacer una ofrenda. La base, cerrada por una puerta de chapa metálica, se remonta a sus estudios del ojo humano. El fuste actúa como un reloj de sol, proyectando su sombra sobre la plataforma circular; la base de ésta se encuentra revestida de un mosaico de azulejos fragmentados que recuerda al Parque Güell de Antonio Gaudí. Estrechamente ligada a su situación geográfica, la Torre de Montjuic es un símbolo no sólo de los Juegos Olímpicos, sino también de la historia de Barcelona, marcada por el arte y el espíritu de progreso.

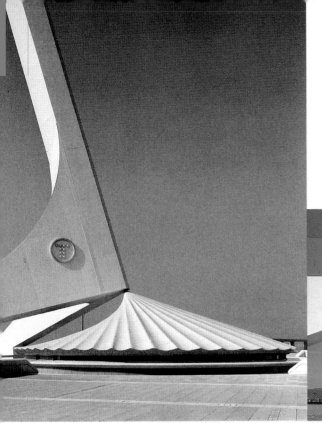

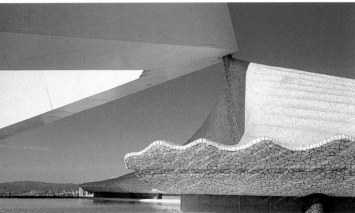

Erigida perto do Palau Sant Jordi, obra do arquitecto japonês Arata Isozaki, a Torre de Comunicações de Montjuic tem 130 m de altura. Como o seu vizinho, foi construída por ocasião dos Jogos Olímpicos de 1992, sendo composta por um tronco inclinado, no cimo do qual se fixou um importante elemento semicircular. Embora sugira um dardo, foi beber a sua inspiração a um esboço de Calatrava que representa uma figura humana em posição de oferenda. A base, cerrada por uma porta feita de lâminas metálicas, aponta para os seus estudos sobre o olho humano. Qual agulha de um relógio solar, o tronco projecta uma sombra sobre a plataforma circular inferior. Esta encontra-se coberta de azulejos partidos, recordando o Parque Güell de Antoni Gaudí. Estreitamente arraigada na geografia e orientação do local, a Torre de Montjuic simboliza os Jogos Olímpicos e também a história da cidade de Barcelona, marcada pela arte e pelo espírito do progresso.

La torre delle telecomunicazioni di Montjuic si erge a un'altezza di 130 m non lontano dal Palau Sant Jordi, progettato dall'architetto giapponese Arata Isozaki. Costruita come il suo vicino in occasione delle Olimpiadi del 1992, consta di un fusto inclinato sul quale si innesta, in posizione elevata, un elemento semicircolare. Anche se può ricordare un giavellotto, la torre si basa in realtà su un disegno di Calatrava che mostra una figura inginocchiata mentre porge un'offerta. Anche il basamento, con una porta in lame di metallo, è ispirato dai suoi studi sull'occhio umano. Il fusto funziona come la lancetta di una meridiana, proiettando l'ombra sulla piattaforma circolare sottostante. Il rivestimento di piastrelle a mosaico di quest'ultima suscita associazioni con il Parque Güell di Antoni Gaudí. Strettamente correlata alla posizione geografica e all'orientamento solare del sito, la torre di Montjuic è simbolo non soltanto dei Giochi Olimpici ma anche della storia di Barcellona, città d'arte e contrassegnata da uno spirito progressista.

Montjuic Communications Tower,
Barcelona, Spain, 1989–92

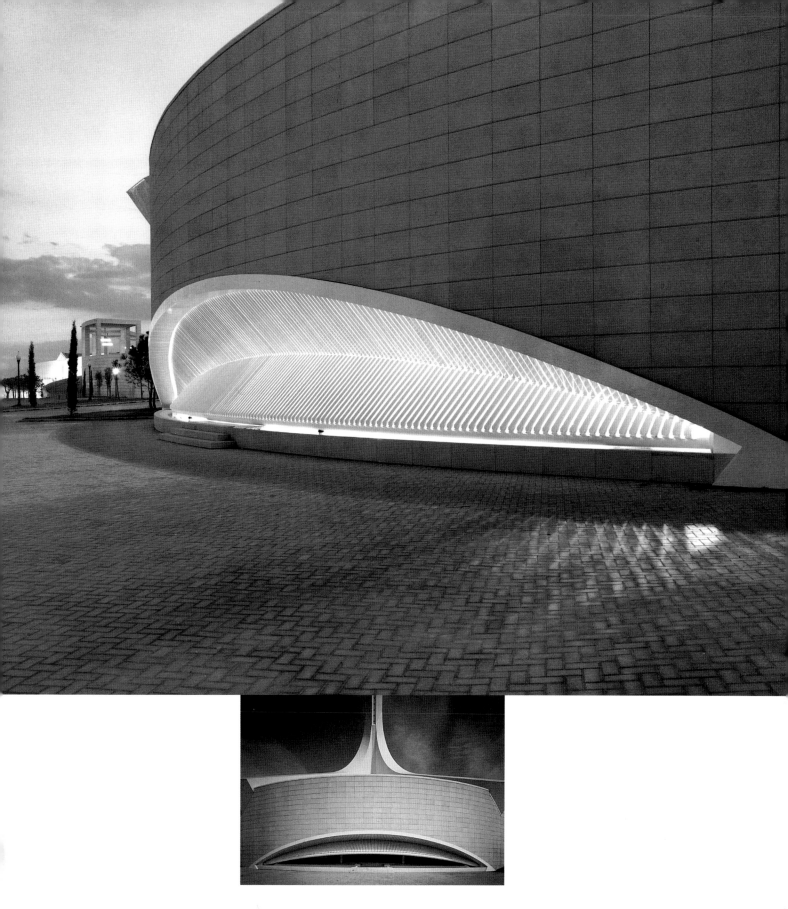

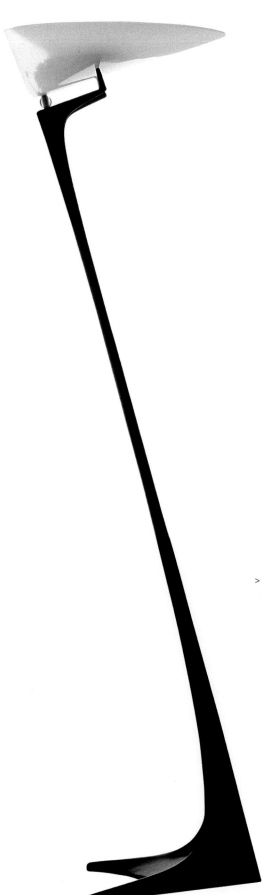

> Montjuic Communications Tower – "Génesis de la forme"

Estos grafics del cuerpo

Síntesis de la forma

expresión de los pies
eventualmente esculturas de giacometti

La nueva estación de Lisboa forma parte del ambicioso plan de urbanismo iniciado con ocasión de la Exposición Universal de 1998 en la capi
portuguesa; se encuentra situada a unos cinco kilómetros del centro histórico, a orillas del Tajo. El aspecto más espectacular del proyecto es,
sin duda, la cubierta, de 78 metros por 238, que se extiende sobre las ocho vías y que recuerda un bosque. En lugar de subrayar la ruptura
entre la ciudad y el río que supone la estación, Calatrava intentó aquí, como en muchos otros proyectos, abrir conexiones y reestablecer las
relaciones. El complejo incluye dos grandes marquesinas metálicas y acristaladas sobre las zonas de acceso, de no menos de 112 metros por
El proyecto de Calatrava incluye también una estación de autobuses, un aparcamiento, una estación de metro y una galería longitudinal con
zonas comerciales. La venta de billetes y demás servicios se encuentran a 5 metros por debajo de los andenes, con un pórtico que marca
la galería comercial que se encuentra a esa profundidad; la entrada junto al río desempeña el papel de acceso principal.

Enquanto parte de um ambicioso plano de urbanização envolvendo a Exposição Universal em 1998 na capital portuguesa, esta nova estação situa-se a cinco quilómetros do centro da cidade, perto do rio Tejo. O pormenor mais espectacular deste projecto é a cobertura, com 78 por 238 m de superfície, sobre as oito vias férreas sobrelevadas, cujos pilares poderão evocar a tipologia de uma floresta. Mais do que acentuar a ruptura entre a cidade e o rio que circunda a estação, Calatrava procurou, como é hábito, abrir caminhos e restabelecer ligações. O complexo inclui, sob as aberturas, dois grandes telheiros em vidro e aço medindo nada menos que 112 por 11 m. Poder-se-á encontrar também uma estação rodoviária, um parque automóvel, uma estação de metro subterrânea e uma galeria comercial longitudinal – um conjunto totalmente previsto no caderno de encargos. As instalações de acolhimento e de venda de bilhetes situam-se a cinco metros abaixo do nível das vias, com um átrio anunciando a galeria comercial cinco metros mais abaixo, e a abertura do lado do rio funciona como acesso principal.

La nuova stazione ferroviaria di Lisbona, situata a circa 5 km dal centro storico, non lontano dal fiume Tago, è stata realizzata nell'ambito di un ambizioso programma urbanistico varato in occasione dell'Esposizione Universale del 1998. L'aspetto più spettacolare del progetto è senza dubbio la copertura (con una superficie di 78 x 238 m) che si estende sopra gli otto binari sopraelevati e che suggerisce l'impressione di una foresta. Come in altri suoi lavori, anche qui Calatrava ha mirato ad aprire dei passaggi e a stabilire un collegamento tra la città e il fiume, invece di accentuare la frattura rappresentata dalla stazione. Al di sopra delle aperture si sviluppano due grandi tettoie in vetro e acciaio, lunghe 112 m e larghe 11. Il progetto include una stazione degli autobus, un parcheggio, una stazione della metropolitana sotterranea e un centro commerciale sviluppato longitudinalmente. La biglietteria e gli altri servizi si trovano 5 m sotto i binari, mentre altri 5 m più sotto è situato l'atrio. L'apertura sul lato del fiume costituisce l'accesso principale.

Oriente Station,
Lisbon, Portugal, 1993–98

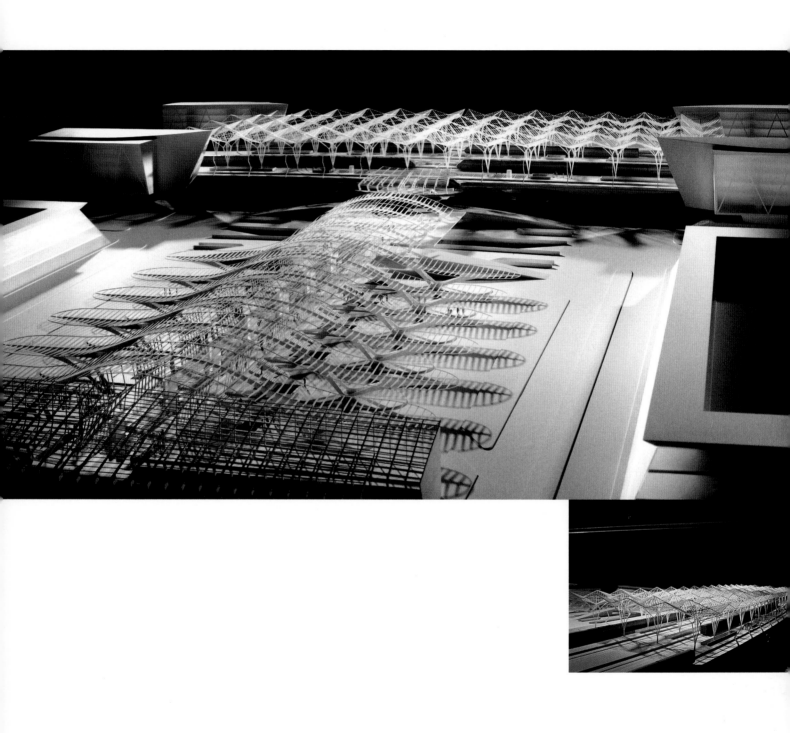

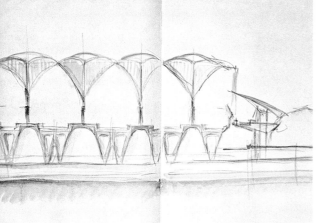

Ondarroa es un pequeño puerto de mar vasco, en la desembocadura del río Artibay, no lejos de Bilbao. El puente de Santiago Calatrava, con un solo arco inclinado, actúa como puerta de entrada a la ciudad; sus etéreas líneas contrastan fuertemente con las densas construcciones modernas que se extienden a lo largo de la curva que describe la avenida marítima. El puente tiene una luz de 71,5 metros y una anchura que varía de 20,9 a 23,7 metros. Esta construcción de acero posee una calzada peatonal curva poco usual, mientras que la calzada principal, de 11 metros, es recta; de este modo, en el centro, entre la circulación rodada y los peatones, queda un vacío considerable. Los peatones que desean cruzar el puente rápidamente pueden utilizar el carril situado al otro lado del puente. Los perfiles inclinados que sustentan la calzada peatonal se encuentran reforzados cada 2,86 metros por puntales de acero radiales y por fuertes cables dobles verticales anclados a la calzada principal. Este puente, con los de Valencia y Orléans, constituyen la nueva tipología de Calatrava, que se caracteriza por poseer una estructura horizontal que sirve de tensor del sistema, lo que le permite resistir distorsiones y reducir las deformaciones por tensión al mínimo. Con este sistema también es posible situar el arco asimétricamente.

Ondarroa é um pequeno porto de mar, situado na foz do rio Artibay sobre a costa basca, perto de Bilbau. Esta ponte, com um arco único inclinado, funciona como porta de entrada para a cidade, e o seu perfil aéreo e nervoso contrasta com a disposição dos edifícios modernos que forram a curva do rio. O perfil do arco em aço parece arredar para o lado uma invulgar passagem para peões em curva, contrário ao tabuleiro principal com 11 m de largura, o qual é rectilíneo, possuindo um grande vácuo ao centro, entre a circulação dos veículos e a dos peões. Os transeuntes que prefiram fazer um caminho mais directo podem sempre recorrer ao passeio que ladeia a estrada. Cabos de aço irradiantes, colocados a cada 2,86 m, sustêm o arco e a passagem para peões curva, sendo que o tabuleiro da estrada está seguro por sólidos cabos duplos verticais. Tal ponte, como aquelas de Valência e de Orleães, revela uma tipologia desenvolvida recentemente por Calatrava, em que a estrutura portante horizontal tem um efeito retesador sobre o sistema estrutural, permitindo-lhe resistir aos embargos da torção e minimizar a deformação por torção. Este sistema possibilita ao arco adoptar uma posição assimétrica em relação ao tabuleiro.

Ondarroa è un piccolo porto di mare situato alle foci dell'Artibay, sulla costa basca della Spagna, non lontano da Bilbao. Il ponte di Santiago Calatrava, con il suo singolo arco inclinato, funziona un po' da porta d'accesso alla città, e il suo profilo aereo e nervoso contrasta con il fitto allineamento di edifici moderni che fronteggiano l'ansa del fiume. Ha una luce di 71,5 m e una larghezza tra i 20,9 e i 23,7 m. Il grande arco in acciaio è costeggiato da un lato da un singolare passaggio pedonale curvo, dall'altro dal piano stradale rettilineo, largo 11 m; viene così a crearsi un vasto spazio vuoto tra il traffico veicolare e il flusso pedonale. I pedoni, se preferiscono una via più diretta, possono in alternativa percorrere il marciapiede che corre lungo la strada. Tiranti d'acciaio radiali posti a una distanza di 2,86 m l'uno dall'altro sostengono l'arco e la passerella curva, mentre l'impalcato è sorretto da potenti doppi cavi che si dipartono verticalmente dall'arco. Questo ponte, come quelli di Valencia e di Orleans, rientra in una tipologia recentemente messa a punto da Calatrava.

Nuevo acceso al puerto de Ondarroa,
Ondarroa, Spain, 1989–95

La decisión de construir el Reichstag al este de la Königsplatz berlinesa se tomó en 1871, pero no comenzaría a construirse sino diez años más tarde, bajo la dirección de Paul Wallot y no del arquitecto que ganó el concurso primero, Friedrich Bohnstedt. En junio de 1992 tuvo lugar un nuevo concurso, casi tan controvertido como el original, con el fin de rehabilitar el edificio, que se encontraba en bastante mal estado de conservación después de haber sufrido un incendio y las consecuencias de la guerra. Los tres ganadores de la primera fase —el holandés Pi De Bruijn (un primer premio inesperado), Sir Norman Foster y Santiago Calatrava— fueron requeridos a finales de abril de 1993 a que reelaboraran sus proyectos. Calatrava fue el que más se acercó en la primera fase a la solución definitiva: su cúpula de 18 metros sobre la Sala de Plenos, extremadamente ligera, era muy similar al proyecto final de Foster, que ganó el concurso. La cúpula de Calatrava estaba prevista para abrirse y cerrarse, una característica extraordinaria para una estructura que actúa en tensión y no a compresión. Su proyecto preveía vaciar cuidadosamente el edificio y diseñar los espacios interiores lo más diáfanos y luminosos posible. Para evitar que el interior resultase recargado, propuso crear un nuevo edificio de oficinas para los grupos parlamentarios. Este proyecto, denominado Dorotheenblock, será construido ahora por el holandés Pi de Bruijn.

Remonta a 1871 a decisão de construir o Reichstag na extremidade leste da Königsplatz, mas seria Paul Wallot, e não o vencedor inicial do concurso, Friedrich Bohnstedt, que inauguraria os trabalhos de construção dez anos mais tarde. Em Junho de 1992, foi lançado um outro concurso, com resultados quase tão controversos quanto o primeiro, para restaurar o edifício gravemente danificado por um incêndio histórico e pela guerra. Foi solicitado aos três primeiros arquitectos apurados, o inesperado holandês Pi de Bruijn, Norman Foster e Santiago Calatrava, que repensassem as suas propostas iniciais até ao final de Abril de 1993, embora Calatrava estivesse mais próximo da solução definitiva. A sua cúpula delicada com 18 m de abertura sobre a sala das sessões era aparentemente muito semelhante ao projecto final apresentado pelo vencedor do concurso, Foster. A cúpula de Calatrava abrir-se-ia e fechar-se-ia, concepção rara para uma estrutura que funciona por tensão e não por compressão. Neste projecto, a estrutura original do Reichstag era cuidadosamente despida de enfeites, e os espaços interiores deveriam ser também tão purificados e luminosos quanto possível. Para evitar sobrecarregar o interior, Calatrava propusera a criação de um novo bloco de escritórios para os deputados, na parte traseira do Reichstag. Esta área, a qual denominara Dorotheenblock, será construída por Pi de Bruijn.

Risale al 1871 la decisione di costruire il Reichstag sul lato orientale della Königsplatz a Berlino, ma i lavori iniziarono soltanto dieci anni dopo sotto la guida di Paul Wallot, subentrato al primo vincitore del concorso, Friedrich Bohnstedt. Nel giugno 1992 è stato indetto un altro concorso, controverso quasi quanto il primo, per ripristinare l'edificio, che conserva una forte carica simbolica, danneggiato da un grave incendio e dalla guerra. Alla fine dell'aprile del 1993 ai primi tre architetti selezionati – l'olandese Pi de Bruijn (una scelta inattesa), Sir Norman Foster e Santiago Calatrava – venne chiesto di modificare le loro proposte originali, ma era stato fin dall'inizio Calatrava a trovare la soluzione poi adottata: la sua cupola superleggera a coronamento della sala dell'assemblea plenaria, con un'apertura di 18 m, era molto simile a quella in seguito proposta dal vincitore del concorso, Foster, nella versione rielaborata del progetto. Secondo la concezione di Calatrava la struttura originale del Reichstag sarebbe rimasta completamente spoglia e gli spazi interni sarebbero stati quanto più essenziali e luminosi possibile. Per evitare di sovraccaricare l'interno, aveva proposto di creare dietro al Reichstag un nuovo edificio che ospitasse gli uffici dei rappresentanti dei partiti. Questa struttura, da lui denominata Dorotheenblock, verrà ora realizzata da Pi de Bruijn.

Reichstag Conversion,
Berlin, Germany, 1992

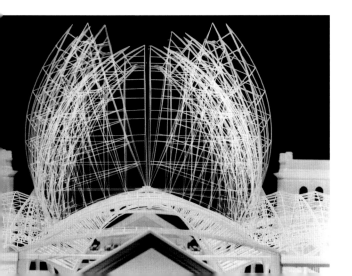

Reichstag Conversion, Berlin, Germany   122 ◂ 123

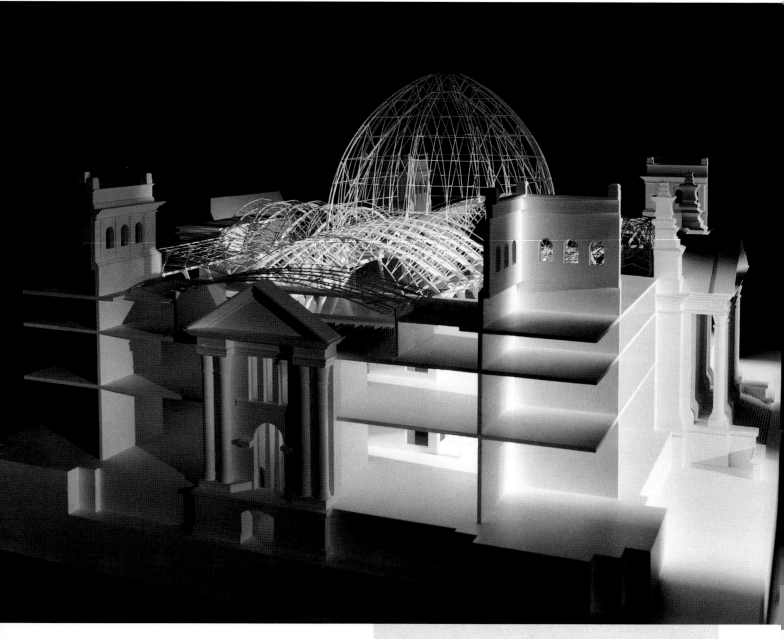

Con una longitud total de 129 metros y dos arcos inclinados y desdoblados, este puente fue uno de los primeros que contribuyó a crear la fama de Santiago Calatrava. Franquea una especie de tierra de nadie que se extiende entre las líneas de ferrocarril y une las calles Bach de Roda y Felipe II, conectando de nuevo un amplio sector de la ciudad con el mar. Esta forma tan característica contribuye a probar la teoría de Calatrava, según la cual las zonas urbanas periféricas pueden recuperarse mediante gestos simbólicos de este tipo. Con una combinación del hormigón para los soportes y el acero para el arco, que parece adelgazar con la altura, el puente Bach de Roda-Felipe II demuestra igualmente la jerarquía de materiales y formas que emplea Calatrava en función de su distancia al suelo. Aunque tiene una estructura diferente, la estación del Aeropuerto de Lyón-Satolas emplea una jerarquía similar.

Esta ponte, com um comprimento total de 129 m e arcos geminados inclinados e abertos, foi uma das primeiras a contribuir para a reputação de Santiago Calatrava. Atravessando uma espécie de terra de ninguém, que nasceu originalmente com a criação de uma via férrea, liga as ruas Bach de Roda e Felipe II e estabelece uma nova relação entre grande parte da cidade e o mar. A sua forma reconhecível testemunha o valor da teoria do arquitecto, segundo a qual as zonas urbanas periféricas podem ser recuperadas através de intervenções simbólicas deste género. Pela combinação de poderosos suportes em betão e uma estrutura em arco metálico, que estreita à medida que se eleva, a obra demonstra igualmente a preferência de Calatrava pela hierarquia das formas e dos materiais, em função da distância do solo. Embora a natureza da sua estrutura seja muito diferente, a estação de Lyon-Satolas recorre a uma hierarquia similar.

Con una lunghezza complessiva di 129 m e due archi gemelli inclinati e spezzati, questo ponte è uno dei primi lavori di Santiago Calatrava che ha contribuito ad affermarne la reputazione. Superando una sorta di «terra di nessuno» creata dalla presenza dei binari ferroviari, esso collega le vie Bach de Roda e Felipe II, riconnettendo in tal modo al mare una vasta zona della città. La sua forma immediatamente riconoscibile suffraga la validità della teoria di Calatrava secondo cui un intervento simbolico di questo genere è in grado di restituire un'individualità ad aree urbane periferiche. Inoltre, con il suo abbinamento di potenti piloni in calcestruzzo e di una struttura ad arco in metallo che diventa sempre più aerea via via che si eleva, il ponte Bach de Roda–Felipe II dimostra come Calatrava si attenga a una gerarchia di materiali e forme, scelti in rapporto alla loro distanza dal terreno. Anche se la sua concezione strutturale è molto diversa, la stazione ferroviaria di Lione-Satolas è basata su una gerarchia di questo tipo.

Bach De Roda–Felipe II Bridge,
Barcelona, Spain, 1984–87

Tota del puent de Barcelona

Tota del puent de Mérido

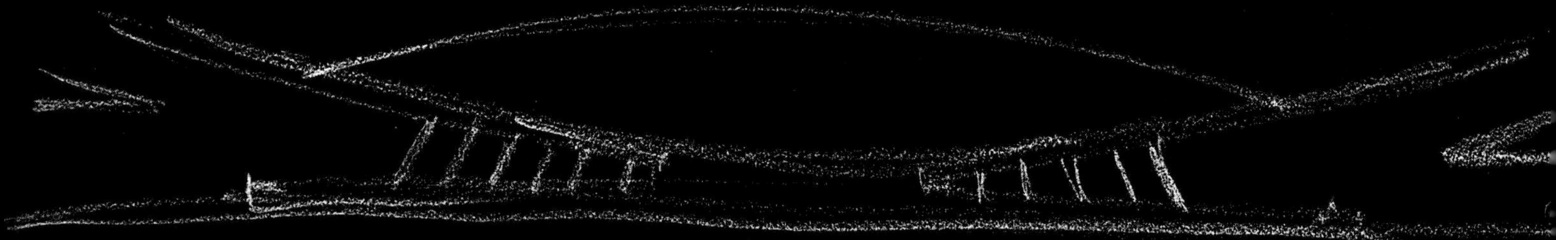

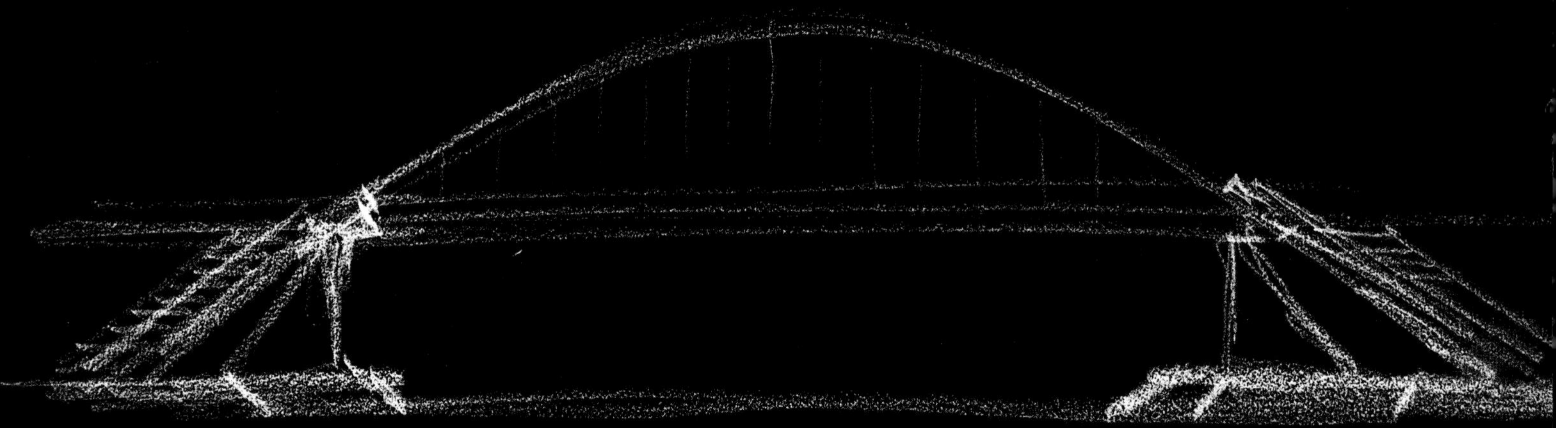

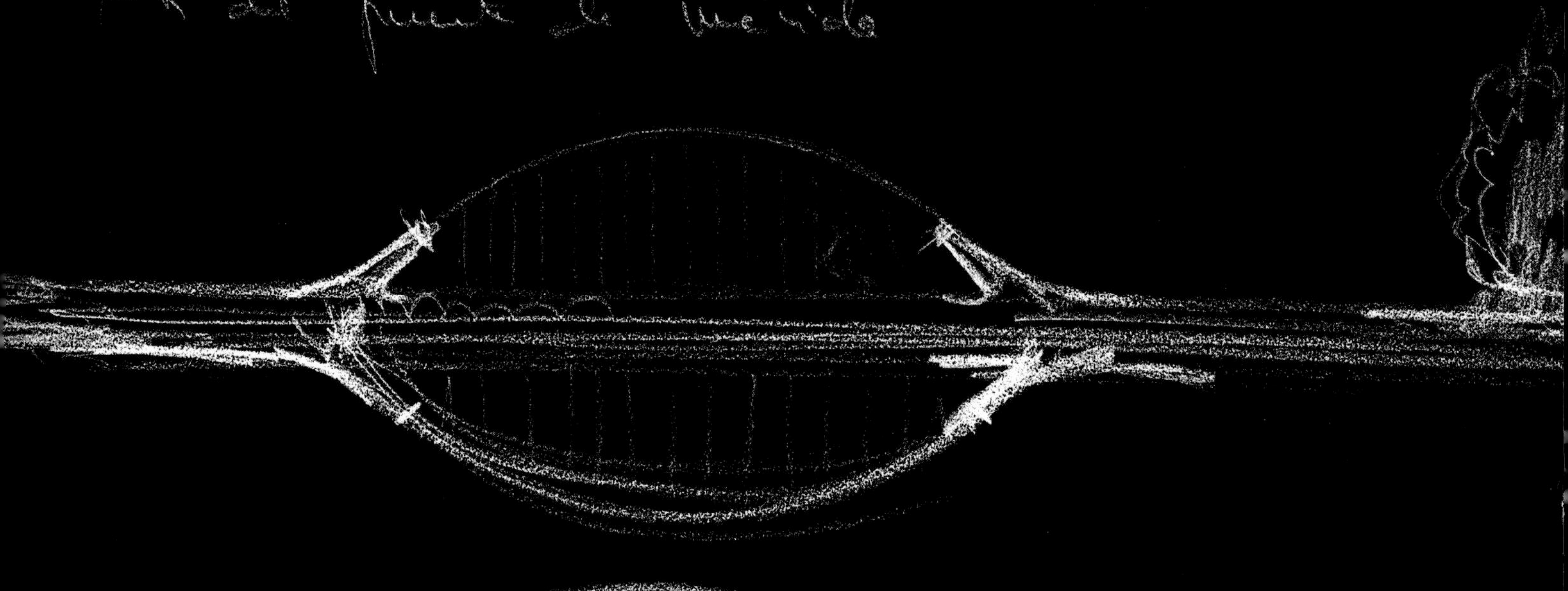

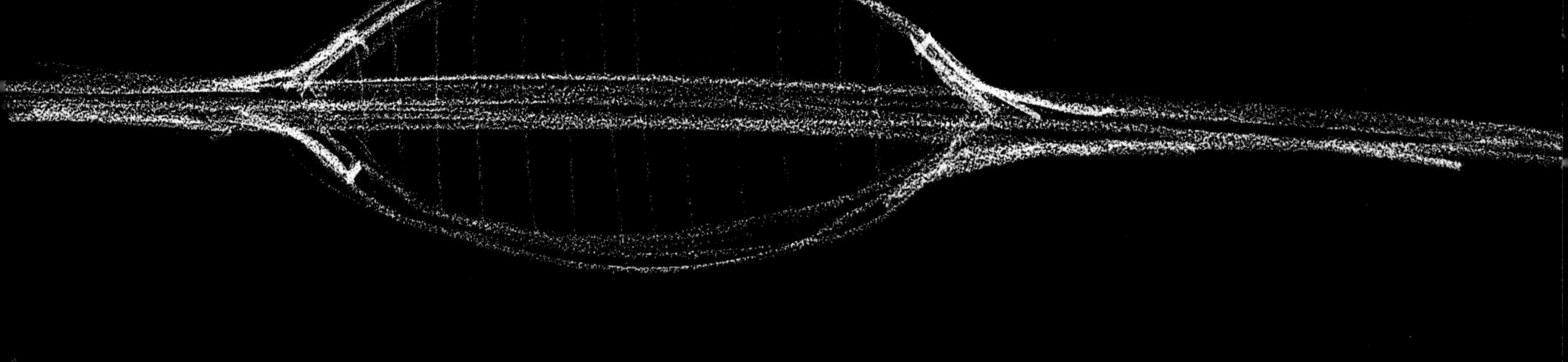

Fue el hecho de ganar este concurso lo que movió a Calatrava a abrir su estudio en Zúrich. La estación de Stadelhofen linda con un terreno en declive, que traza una amplia curva, cerca de la Bellevue Platz y no lejos de la Theater-Strasse, y se encuentra próxima al centro de la ciudad y al Lago de Zúrich. Se extiende a lo largo de unos 270 metros de longitud (y 40 de anchura); su estructura sólo se revela cuando el viajero sale al andén. La primera señal visible de la estación, después de acercarse a ella a través de varias zonas peatonales, es un edificio del siglo XIX, que se ha conservado por su significación en el contexto local. En el subsuelo, una zona comercial paralela; su bóveda nervada de hormigón presenta formas antropomorfas y sigue la curva de los andenes mismos. A la zona comercial se desciende por accesos en forma de boca. Aunque podría dar la impresión de haberse inspirado en una especie de «dinosaurio», los dibujos preparatorios de Calatrava revelan que los pilares inclinados siguen la forma de la mano humana.

Uma das razões por que Santiago Calatrava decidiu abrir o seu escritório em Zurique foi a encomenda que conquistou para a construção desta estação. Situada num talude curvilíneo e arborizado, perto da Bellevue-Platz e da Theater-Strasse, a estação de Stadelhofen não fica longe do centro da cidade e do lago de Zurique. Estende-se por cerca de 270 m (com uma largura de 40 m), e não revela a sua estrutura ao passageiro até este chegar à via férrea propriamente dita. É acessível através de uma série de passagens para peões e o primeiro sinal visível da sua presença é um edifício do século XIX, preservado pelo seu significado para contexto local. No subsolo, um centro comercial, cujas abóbadas estriadas poderão parecer antropomórficas, desenvolve-se paralelamente à curva das linhas. Os acessos em forma de boca permitem descer até esta zona. Os esboços preparatórios de Calatrava não revelam quaisquer traços de dinossauro, mas sim uma mão humana, cuja forma adoptou para conceber as suas colunas inclinadas.

È stato in seguito alla vittoria del concorso per questa stazione che Calatrava ha aperto il suo studio a Zurigo. Incuneata nel fianco di un lieve pendio ricoperto di vegetazione nei pressi di Bellevue-Platz e non lontano da Theater-Strasse, la stazione di Stadelhofen è vicina al centro città e al lago di Zurigo. Si estende per una lunghezza di 270 m circa (con una larghezza di 40 m) e il viaggiatore si rende conto della sua struttura solo quando si trova lungo i binari. Si arriva alla stazione attraverso una serie di vie pedonali e il suo primo segno visibile è un edificio ottocentesco, che è stato conservato e ristrutturato in quanto presenza significativa nel contesto locale. Al livello sotterraneo, seguendo la curva dei binari, si sviluppa un centro commerciale la cui configurazione a nervature di cemento può sembrare antropomorfica. Gli accessi attraverso cui si raggiunge la zona commerciale sono grandi aperture mobili «a bocca». Dai disegni preparatori è evidente che Calatrava non s'ispira affatto a un dinosauro, ma prende piuttosto spunto dalla forma di una mano, da lui adottata per le colonne inclinate.

Stadelhofen Railway Station,
Zurich, Switzerland, 1983–90

- le expresión de las manos
Parcours de la tragicastichement
el gesto -

Stadelhofen Railway Station, Zurich, Switzerland   134 ◄ 135

Aunque podría hacer pensar en una especie de pájaro prehistórico, la forma de esta estación de 5.600 metros cuadrados —construida por los ferrocarriles franceses (SNCF) para conectar la red de trenes de alta velocidad (TGV) con el Aeropuerto de Satolas— está más relacionada con las esculturas de Calatrava que con cualquier animal. Las alas parecen remitir a la TWA Terminal en el Kennedy Airport (1957–1962), obra de Eero Saarinen, pero su función y diversos aspectos, como sus andenes cubiertos de 500 metros de longitud, la diferencian claramente de su predecesora. Construida en tres fases, con un coste total de 600 millones de francos, la estación alberga seis vías; las dos centrales están cubiertas de una estructura reticular de hormigón, para permitir la circulación de trenes de alta velocidad a más de 300 kilómetros por hora. Un puente de 180 metros de longitud conecta la estación con la terminal del aeropuerto, dando al conjunto una forma que recuerda tanto un pájaro como una manta raya. La particularidad esencial es, sin embargo, el vestíbulo principal, con una cubierta de 1.300 toneladas de peso, 120 metros de longitud, 100 de anchura y 40 de altura.

Ainda que faça recordar um qualquer pássaro pré-histórico, a forma deste edifício com 5600 m^2, concebido para a SNCF com a finalidade de ligar a rede do comboio a alta velocidade (TGV) ao Aeroporto de Lyon-Satolas, está mais próxima das esculturas de Calatrava que de algum animal. O desenho em asa recorda igualmente o terminal da TWA construído por Eero Saarinen no Aeroporto Kennedy (1957–1962), mas a sua função e outros aspectos, como a plataforma coberta com 500 m de comprimento, diferenciam-na radicalmente do seu predecessor. Erigida em três fases, com um custo total de 600 milhões de francos, a estação cobre seis vias, das quais as duas ao centro, reservadas aos comboios a alta velocidade, estão isoladas por uma concha em betão. Uma ponte com 180 m de comprimento liga estas instalações ao terminal do aeroporto e confere ao seu plano uma fisionomia comparável a uma raia ou a um pássaro. A sua particularidade essencial consiste no vestíbulo principal coberto por um tecto com 1300 toneladas, medindo 120 m de comprimento por 100 m de largura, para uma altura máxima de 40 m.

Nonostante l'evidente somiglianza con una sorta di uccello preistorico, la forma di questo complesso di 5600 m^2 – progettato per le ferrovie francesi (SNCF) con l'obiettivo di creare un collegamento tra la rete di treni ad alta velocità (TGV) e l'aeroporto lionese di Satolas – è più strettamente associata alle sculture di Calatrava che a un animale qualsiasi. Il profilo che ricorda un uccello sul punto di spiccare il volo richiama il terminal della TWA realizzato da Eero Saarinen al Kennedy Airport (1957–62), ma la sua funzione e gli elementi come i marciapiedi coperti dei binari, lunghi 500 m, differenziano decisamente questo progetto dal suo predecessore. Costruita in tre fasi con un costo totale di 600 milioni di franchi, la stazione ospita sei binari, di cui i due centrali racchiusi in un guscio di cemento e riservati ai treni in transito. Una passerella lunga 180 m, che assicura il collegamento tra l'edificio e il terminal dell'aeroporto, assegna alla planimetria una forma che potrebbe far pensare a una manta o anche a un uccello. L'elemento più cospicuo rimane comunque il salone principale, con una superficie di 120 x 100 m, un'altezza massima di 40 m e una copertura del peso di 1300 tonnellate.

Lyon-Satolas Airport Railway Station,
Lyon, France, 1989–94

Lyon-Satolas Airport Railway Station, Lyon, France   140 ◂ 141

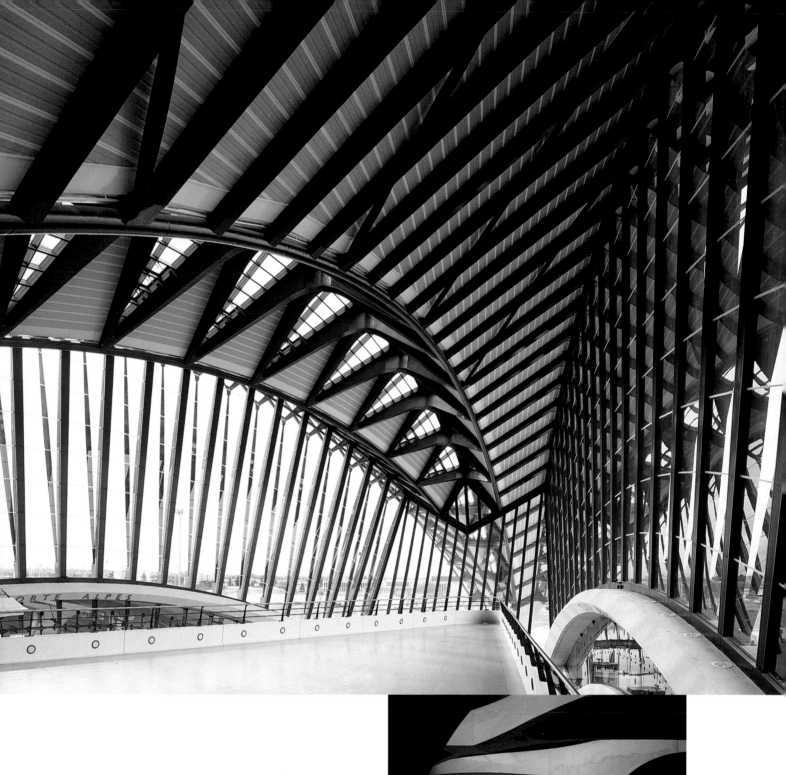

el ojo avido

mira certero, preciso, incisivo

el instrumento físico organo

e orden en consideración de la esto-la

la estima del arquitecto se

su opinión fue s la puente deaccep.

al mundo de las ideas cuya expasíon

splenta e immediata s el gesto de

el ojo de bue

el exte

el ojo de a

el interior   doojaregres

el orden de la intuicion; el orden del pensaminto

consideran ucan otra imagen juzga y controla

aquella, mebidos y precibidos pro el

ideas   ←   →   extenso

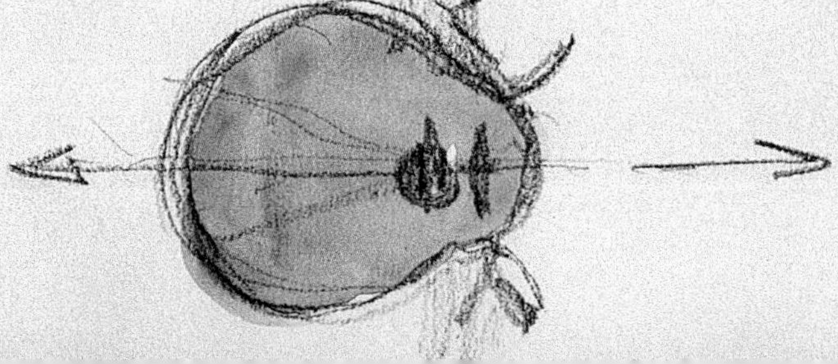

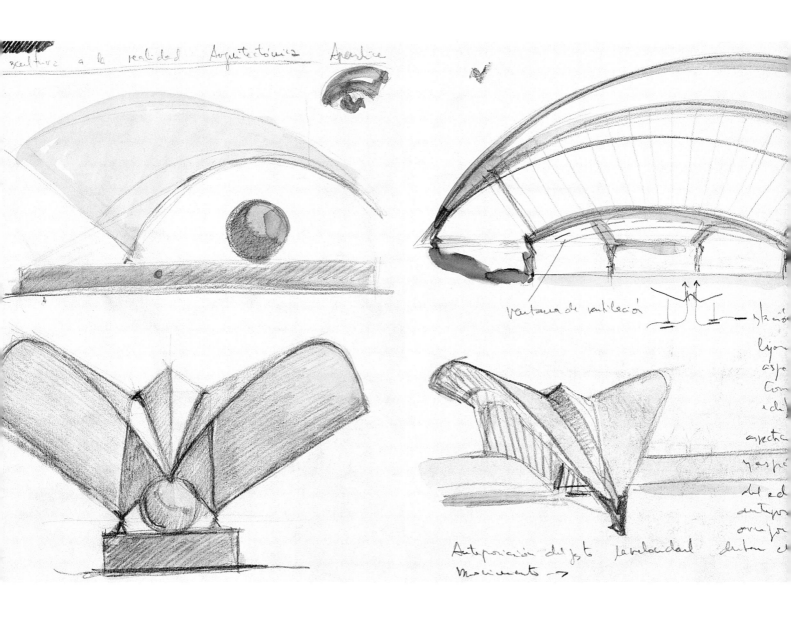

Como muchos otros proyectos recientes de Santiago Calatrava, este puente peatonal de 78,5 metros de longitud y una luz máxima de 54 metros, alcanza un equilibrio notable y una simplicidad extrema. Un mástil de 41 metros de longitud, inclinado 30 grados con respecto a la vertical, sostiene la pasarela, que se abre en forma de Y. El diámetro del mástil varía entre 550 milímetros y 1,22 metros en el punto más ancho. Financiado por la Consejería de Medio Ambiente de Salford City, Chapel Wharf (un área de rehabilitación urbana del antiguo puerto de Manchester) y por el Fondo Europeo de Desarrollo Regional, este puente forma parte de una zona libre de tráfico rodado, a pesar de que está exactamente intercalado entre dos puentes destinados al tráfico de automóviles. Los cables que soportan el puente y la inclinación del mástil recuerdan a ciertos dibujos de Calatrava sobre el cuerpo humano en movimiento. Situado cerca de la Trinity Church, cruza el río Irwel, uniendo a Manchester con la ciudad de Salford.

Como no caso de numerosos projectos recentes de Calatrava, esta ponte para peões, com 78,5 m de comprimento para uma abertura central de 54 m, parece ter atingido um estado de equilíbrio perfeito e uma simplicidade extrema. O pilão, com 41 m de altura e inclinado a 30° em relação à vertical, sustém o tabuleiro que se abre em Y. O diâmetro do pilão varia entre os 550 mm aos 1,22 m. Financiada pelo Departamento do Ambiente, a cidade de Salford, Chapel Wharf (um programa de renovação urbana das antigas docas de Manchester) e o Fundo Europeu para o Desenvolvimento Regional, esta ponte inscreve-se numa zona interdita à circulação automóvel, ainda que se encontre intercalada por duas pontes reservadas a viaturas. Os cabos que suportam o tabuleiro e o ângulo de inclinação do pilão evocam alguns desenhos do arquitecto sobre o movimento do corpo humano. Situada perto da Trinity Church, a ponte para peões atravessa o rio Irwel, ligando Manchester à cidade de Salford.

Come molti progetti recenti di Santiago Calatrava, anche questa passerella pedonale – lunga 78,5 m e con una luce massima di 54 m – sembra mostrare un notevole grado di equilibrio e una semplicità estrema. L'impalcato, che si divarica formando una Y, è sostenuto da un pilone lungo 41 m, inclinato di 30 gradi rispetto alla verticale, con un diametro che varia dai 55 ai 122 cm. Finanziato dal Department of the Environment, dalla Città di Salford, dal Chapel Wharf (un programma di rinnovamento urbano dei «docks» dismessi di Manchester) e dal Fondo europeo di sviluppo regionale, la passerella è inclusa in una zona destinata a essere chiusa al traffico veicolare, per quanto si trovi tra due ponti carrozzabili. I cavi che sostengono l'impalcato e l'angolo di inclinazione del pilone rinviano senz'altro ai disegni di Calatrava sul tema del corpo umano in movimento. Situata nei pressi della Trinity Church, la passerella attraversa il fiume Irwel, creando un collegamento tra Manchester e Salford.

Trinity Bridge,
Salford, England, 1993–95

Este arco parabólico inclinado posee una luz de 71 metros. Los montantes verticales de acero que van del arco a la pasarela, cada 5,7 metros, proporcionan la impresión de un movimiento suspendido, una especie de péndulo (como ha sugerido Sergio Polano). La pasarela une el casco urbano de Bilbao con la degradada área industrial de Urbitarte, atravesando la ría de Bilbao. La pasarela del Campo Volantín forma parte de un amplio programa de rehabilitación urbana que incluye el Museo Guggenheim de Bilbao, recientemente construido por Frank Gehry, la nueva línea de metro, diseñada por Sir Norman Foster, y el proyecto del Aeropuerto de Sondica, del propio Calatrava. Como sucede en muchos otros proyectos de Santiago Calatrava, el aparente desequilibrio o, mejor dicho, esa especie de movimiento suspendido queda subrayado por la ligereza de la construcción. La importancia simbólica del puente, que probablemente ejercerá una influencia considerable sobre la reordenación urbana, se realza aún más por la espectacular iluminación nocturna.

Esta estrutura em arco parabólico inclinado apresenta uma abertura de 71 m. As escoras verticais em aço, que ligam o arco ao tabuleiro a cada 5,7 m, criam uma impressão de movimento parado, talvez o de um pêndulo, como sugeriu Sergio Polano. Aproximando um bairro comercial em declínio, denominado Urbitarte, à cidade de Bilbau, do outro lado do rio, esta ponte inscreve-se no âmbito de uma vasta campanha de recuperação urbana, a qual compreende o Guggenheim Bilbao Museum de Frank Gehry, recentemente inaugurado, estações de metro de Norman Foster e o projecto para o aeroporto de Sondica, igualmente da autoria de Calatrava. Como em numerosos outros projectos deste último, o desequilíbrio aparente, ou melhor, a sensação de movimento bloqueado, é sublinhada pela leveza da estrutura. A importância simbólica da ponte, que deverá exercer certamente alguma influência sobre a regeneração urbana desta área, é realçada por uma iluminação nocturna incomparável.

Questo ponte pedonale ad arco parabolico inclinato ha una luce di 71 m. I montanti verticali in acciaio che corrono fra l'arco e l'impalcato a un intervallo di 5,7 m l'uno dall'altro comunicano un'impressione di movimento congelato, simile forse a quello di un «pendolo sospeso nel suo moto», come ha suggerito Sergio Polano. Collegando un'area commerciale dismessa denominata Urbitarte con il centro di Bilbao, dall'altra parte del fiume, il ponte di Campo Volantin rientra nell'ambito di una vasta campagna di rinnovamento urbano che include il Guggenheim Bilbao Museum di Frank O. Gehry, recentemente inaugurato, le stazioni della metropolitana progettate da Sir Norman Foster e le strutture dell'aeroporto di Sondica, sempre di Calatrava. Come in molti altri progetti dell'architetto, l'apparente squilibrio, o piuttosto il senso di movimento congelato, è sottolineato dalla levità della struttura. L'importanza simbolica del ponte, che effettivamente potrebbe esercitare un'influenza sulla riqualificazione ambientale di questa zona, è accentuata da uno spettacolare sistema di illuminazione.

Campo Volantin Footbridge,
Bilbao, Spain, 1990–97

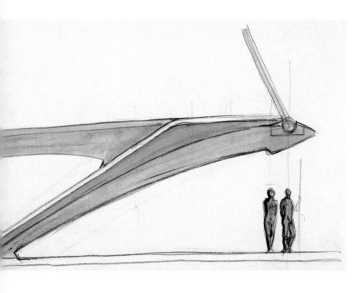

Una de las características frecuentes en los proyectos de Santiago Calatrava es su imprevista capacidad de movimiento. Al igual que sucede con las esculturas que tiene expuestas sobre el césped de su estudio zuriqués, el movimiento se relaciona indudablemente con la fascinación que siente por las formas naturales o antropomorfas. El «movimiento suspendido», tan evidente en varios de sus puentes, va incluso más lejos. Este es el caso de los almacenes Ernsting (Coesfeld, población cercana a Münster, Alemania, 1983–85), con sus tres grandes puertas, de 13 x 5 metros, que recuerdan la articulación de una rodilla humana. Cuando se abre, las «costillas» de aluminio se elevan formando un arco cóncavo que recuerda un dosel. El Pabellón de Kuwait en la Expo 92 de Sevilla (1991–92) integra igualmente el movimiento como una de sus principales características, con 17 «costillas» de madera entrelazada de 25 metros cada una, que se cierran durante el día sobre una plaza, mientras que por la noche se abren para servir de espacio de proyección de diapositivas y vídeo. Otros ejemplos de proyectos con elementos móviles son la ampliación del Museo de Arte de Milwaukee y su «shadow machine» (máquina de las sombras, 1992–93), diseñada para el jardín del Museum of Modern Art de Nueva York.

Una caratteristica ricorrente delle opere di Calatrava è la loro inaspettata capacità di movimento. Come nelle sculture disposte sul prato della sua casa-studio zurighese, questo movimento è indubbiamente collegato alla passione per le forme naturali o antropomorfiche. Il «movimento congelato», evidente per esempio in alcuni dei suoi ponti, in qualche caso diventa un movimento vero e proprio: come nel magazzino Ernsting (Coesfeld, nei pressi di Münster, Germania, 1983–85), le cui tre grandi porte di 13 x 5 m sono state disegnate pensando all'articolazione del ginocchio umano. Le nervature in alluminio che si sollevano per consentire l'accesso formano un arco concavo che costituisce una sorta di baldacchino. Anche il Padiglione del Kuwait all'Expo '92 di Siviglia (1991–92) integra nella sua concezione il movimento, con 17 costoloni in legno, ciascuno della lunghezza di 25 m, che s'intrecciano e si chiudono durante il giorno su una «piazza» che di notte, quando il sistema di copertura mobile è in posizione chiusa, viene usata per proiezioni di video e diapositive. Altri progetti di Calatrava che includono parti mobili sono l'ampliamento del Milwaukee Art Museum e la «Shadow Machine» (1992–93) concepita per il giardino del Museum of Modern Art di New York.

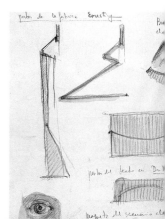

A capacidade de movimento é uma característica constante e inesperada dos projectos de Santiago Calatrava. Como se pode verificar pelas esculturas expostas no relvado do seu estúdio em Zurique, este movimento está indubitavelmente ligado à sua atracção por formas antropomórficas. O «movimento parado», tão evidente em algumas das suas pontes, por exemplo, vai ainda mais longe. É o caso do entreposto Ernsting (Coesfeld, Alemanha, 1983–1985), cujas três grandes portas, medindo 13 por 5 m, foram desenhadas atendendo à articulação do joelho humano. As «costelas» em alumínio abrem-se para cima, moldando um arco côncavo em forma de dossel. O pavilhão do Kuwait na Expo '92 em Sevilha (1991–1982) integrava também o movimento na sua concepção através das suas «costelas» entrelaçadas em madeira, com 25 m de comprimento, que se fechavam durante o dia sobre uma «piazza» e que se abriam à noite proporcionando um espaço de projecção de diaporamas e vídeos. Entre outros projectos de Calatrava com elementos móveis, figuram o alargamento do Milwaukee Art Museum e a sua «Shadow Machine» (Máquina de Sombras, 1992–1993), concebida para o jardim do Museum of Modern Art de Nova Iorque.

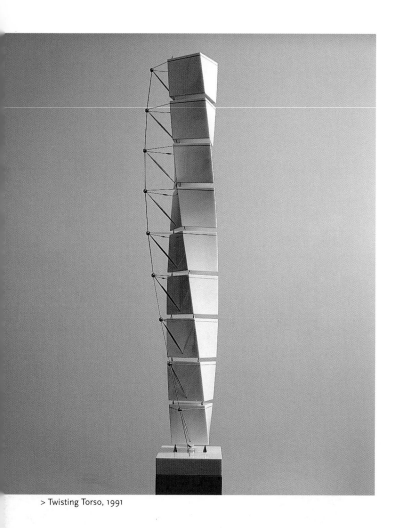

> Twisting Torso, 1991

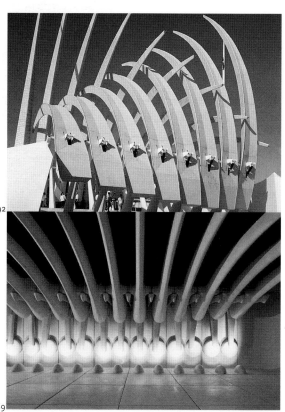

> Kuwait Pavilion, 1992

> Swissbau Concrete Pavilion, 1989

> Fountain

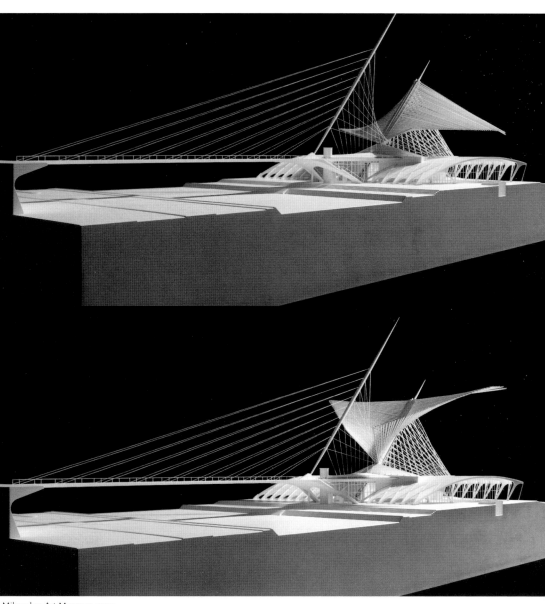

> Milwaukee Art Museum, 2001

Cable-stayed bridge studies, 1979–1981

Acleta Alpine Motor-Bridge, Disentis, Switzerland, 1979

IBA Squash Hall, Berlin, Germany, 1979

Züspa Exhibition Hall, Zurich, Switzerland, 1981

Letten Motorway Bridge, Zurich, Switzerland, 1982

Schwarzhaupt Factory, Dielsdorf, Switzerland, 1982

Mühlenareal Library, Thun, Switzerland, 1982

Rhine Bridge, Diepoldsau, Switzerland, 1982

Thalberg House Balcony Extension, Zurich, Switzerland, 1983–1983

Jakem Steel Warehouse, Munchwilen, Switzerland, 1983–1984

Ernsting's Warehouse, Coesfeld, Germany, 1983–1985

Baumwollhof Balcony, Zurich, Switzerland, 1983–1983

Stadelhofen Railway Station, Zurich, Switzerland, 1983–1990

Post Office Dispatch Roof Canopy, Lucerne, Switzerland, 1983–1985

St. Fiden Bus Stop Shelter, St. Gallen, Switzerland, 1983–1985

Wohlen Highschool, Wohlen, Switzerland, 1983–1988

Lucerne Station Hall, Lucerne, Switzerland, 1983–1989

Bärenmatte Community Centre, Suhr, Switzerland, 1984–1988

Dobi Office Building, Suhr, Switzerland, 1984–1985

De Sede Mobile Exhibition Pavilion, Zurich, Switzerland, 1984

Caballeros Footbridge, Lerida, Spain, 1984

Bach de Roda Bridge, Barcelona, Spain, 1984–1987

Feldenmoos Park & Ride Footbridge, Feldenmoos, Switzerland, 1985

Avenida Diagonal Traffic Signals, Barcelona, Spain, 1986

9 d'Octubre Bridge, Valencia, Spain, 1986–1988

St. Gall Youth Music School Concert Room, St. Gallen, Switzerland, 1986-86

Blackbox Television Studio, Zurich, Switzerland, 1986–1987

Tabourettli Theatre, Basle, Switzerland, 1986–1987

Raitenau Overpass, Salzburg, Austria, 1986

BCE Place: Gallery & Heritage Square, Toronto, Canada, 1987–1992

Oudry-Mesly Footbridge, Créteil-Paris, France, 1987–1988

Passerelle de Thiers, Thiers, France, 1987

Pontevedra Bridge, Pontevedra, Spain, 1987

Basarrate Underground Station, Bilbao, Spain, 1987

Alamillo Bridge and La Cartuja Viaduct, Seville, Spain, 1987–1992

Buchen Housing Estate, Würenlingen, Switzerland, 1987–1996

Banco Exterior, Zurich, Switzerland, 1987–1987

Cascine Footbridge, Florence, Italy, 1987

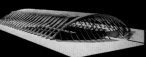

Pré Babel Sports Centre, Geneva, Switzerland, 1988

Leimbach Footbridge, Zurich, Switzerland, 1988

Lusitania Bridge, Merida, Spain, 1988–1991

Collserolla Television Tower, Collserolla Hills, Barcelona, Spain, 1988

Wettstein Bridge, Basle, Switzerland, 1988

Gentil Bridge, Paris, France, 1988

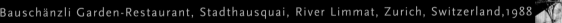

Bauschänzli Garden-Restaurant, Stadthausquai, River Limmat, Zurich, Switzerland, 1988

Emergency Services Centre, Moosbruggstrasse, St. Gallen, Switzerland, 1988–1998

Miraflores Bridge, Cordoba, Spain, 1989

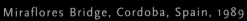

Montjuic Telecommunications Tower, Montjuic Hill, Barcelona, Spain, 1989–1992

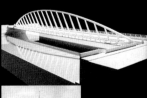

Bahnhofquai Tram Stop, Zurich, Switzerland, 1989

 Reuss Footbridge, Flüelen, Switzerland, 1989

 Swissbau Concrete Pavilion, Muba Exhibition Centre, Basle, Switzerland, 1988–1989

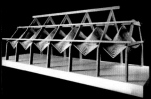 Bohl Covered Bus and Tram Stop, Marktplatz, St. Gall , Switzerland,1989–1996

 Zurich University - Law Faculty Library, Rämi and Zürichbergstrasse, Zurich, Switzerland, 1989

 Muri Cloister Old Age Home, Muri, Switzerland, 1989

Lyon-Satolas Airport Railway Station. Satolas, Lyon, France, 1989–1994

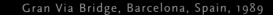 CH-91 Floating Concrete Pavilion. Lake Lucerne, Switzerland, 1989

Gran Via Bridge, Barcelona, Spain, 1989

 Nuevo acceso al puerto de Ondarroa, Ondarroa, Spain, 1989–1995

La Devesa Footbridge. Ripoll, Spain, 1989–1991

Campo Volantin Footbridge, Bilbao, Spain, 1990–1997

Spitalfields Gallery. London, Great Britain, 1990

East London River Crossing, London, England, 1990

eau pont sur le Vecchio Bridge, Corsica, France, 1990

Belluard Castle Theatre, Fribourg, Switzerland, 1990

Sondica Airport, Bilbao, Spain, 1990–2000

Santa Cruz de Tenerife, Canary Islands, Spain, 1991–

Calabria Football Stadium, Reggio Calabria, Italy, 1991
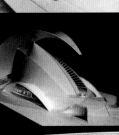

Valencia Communications Tower, Valencia, Spain, 1991

Kuwait Pavilion, Expo'92, Seville, Spain, 1991–1992

Salou Football Stadium, Salou, Tarragona, Spain, 199

Ciudad de las Artes y de las Ciencias, Valencia, Spain

Grand Pont Motorway Bridge, Lille, France, 1991

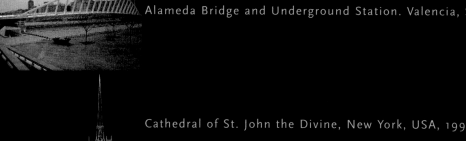

Alameda Bridge and Underground Station. Valencia, S

Cathedral of St. John the Divine, New York, USA, 199

Médoc Swingbridge, Bordeaux, France, 1991

Kronprinzen Bridge, Berlin, Germany, 1991–1996

Beton Forum Standard Bridge, Stockholm, Sweden, 19

Spandau Railway Station, Spandau, Berlin, Germany,

Klosterstrasse Railway Bridge, Berlin, Germany, 1991

Jahn Olympic Sports Complex, Berlin, Germany, 1992

Solferino Footbridge, Paris, France, 1992

London Underground Modular Station, London, England, 1992

Exhibition Hall, Santa Cruz Tenerife, Canary Islands, 1992–1996

Reichstag Conversion, Berlin, Germany, 1992

Serreria Bridge, Valencia, Spain, 1992–

Lake Bridge, Lucerne, Switzerland, 1992

Shadow Machine, Museum of Modern Art New York, 1992–1993

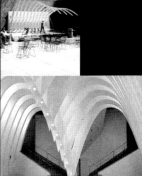

Alcoy Municipal Centre, Alcoy, Spain, 1992–1996

Öresund Bridge, Copenhagen, Denmark, 1993

Ile Falcon Motorway Bridge, Sierre, Switzerland, 1993

Trinity Footbridge, Salford, England, 1993–1995

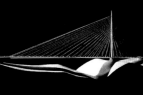

Granadilla Bridge, Tenerife, Spain, 1993

De la Rade Bridge, Geneve, Switzerland, 1993

Telecommunications Tower of Alicante, Alicante, Spain, 1993

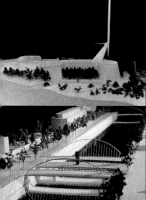

Hospital Bridges, Murcia, Spain, 1993–1999

Sondica Control Tower, Bilbao, Spain, 1993–1996

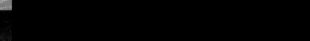

Southpoint Pavilion, New York, USA, 1993

Oriente Station, Lisbon, Portugal, 1993–1998

St. Paul's Bridge, London, England, 1994

Quay Point Pedestrian Bridge, Bristol, England, 1994

Milwaukee Art Museum, Milwaukee, Wisconsin, USA, 1994–2001

Fair and Convention Centre, Fiuggi, Italy, 1994

Worldcup Football Stadium, Marseille, France, 1995

Pedestrian Bridge at Turtle Bay, Redding, USA, 1995–

Zurich Station Platform Roof, Zurich, Switzerland, 1995

Poole Harbour Bridge, Portsmouth, England, 1995

Embankment Renaissance Footbridge, Bedford, England, 1995

Sundsvall Bridge, Sundsvall, Sweden, 1995

Bilbao Football Stadium, Bilbao, Spain, 1995

Quarto Ponte sul Canale Grande, Venice, Italy, 1996–

New Olympic Stadium, Hammerby Waterfront, Stockholm, Sweden, 1996

Church of the Year 2000, Rome, Italy, 1996

Cathedral Square, Los Angeles, USA, 1996

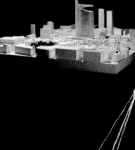

City Point Tower, City of London, England, 1996

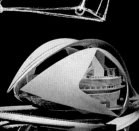

Mimico Creek Pedestrian Bridge, Toronto, Canada, 1996–1998

Palacio de las Artes, Valencia, Spain, 1996–

Service Station / Rest stop, Geneva, Switzerland, 1996–

Liège Guillemins Railway Station, Liège, Belgium, 1997–

Orléans Bridge, Orléans, France, 1996–2000

Port de Barcelona, Barcelona, Spain, 1997

Barajas Airport, Madrid, Spain, 1997

Pfalzkeller Gallery, St. Gallen, Switzerland, 1997–1999

Liège Pedestrian Bridge, Liège, Belgium, 1998–2000

Toronto Island Airport Bridge, Toronto, Canada, 1998

Bodegas Ysios, San Sebastian, Spain, 1998–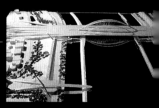

Trinity River Bridge, Dallas, USA, 1998–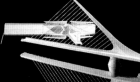

Puerto Madero Pedestrian Bridge, Buenos Aires, Argentina, 1998–

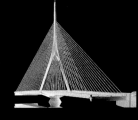

Macken Street & Blackhall Place Bridge, Dublin, Ireland, 1998–

The Corcoran Gallery of Art, Washington, USA, 1999

Turning Torso, Malmö, Sweden, 1999–

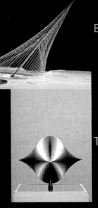

Bridges over the Hoofdvaart, Hoofdorp, Netherlands, 1999–

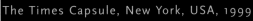

The Times Capsule, New York, USA, 1999

Cruz y Luz, Monterrey, Mexico, 1999–

Leuven Station, Sint-Niklaas, Belgium, 1999

Oakland Diocese Cathedral Campus Projekt, Oakland, USA, 2000–

Buenavista y Jovellanos, Oviedo, Spain, 2000–

Bibliografía > Bibliografia

*Architectures d'ingénieurs,
XIXe-XXe siècles,*
Centre de Création Industrielle
(CCI) du Centre Georges
Pompidou, CCI-Edition, 1978
Billington, David, *Robert Maillart's
Bridges, The Art of Engineering,*
Princeton University Press,
Princeton, New Jersey, 1977
Blanco, Manuel, *Santiago Calatrava.
Exhibition catalogue,* Generalitat
Valenciana, 1999
Cullen, Michael S., Martin Kieren,
*Calatrava Berlin,
Five Projects/Fünf Projekte,*
Photographs by Heinrich
Helfenstein, Birkhäuser, Basel,
Boston, Berlin, 1994
Frampton, Kenneth, Anthony C.
Webster and Anthony Tischhauser,
Calatrava Bridges, Birkhäuser-Verlag,
Basel, Boston, Berlin,
2nd edition, 1996
Giedion, Sigfried, *Space, Time and
Architecture, The Growth of a New
Tradition,* Harvard University Press,
Cambridge, Massachusetts, 1941,
fifth edition, 1976
Glancey, Jonathan, "Calatrava:
a Man with Skeletons in
his Closet," *The Independent,*
October 28, 1992
Glancey, Jonathan, "Passion
Tower," *The Independent, Tabloid,*
December 6, 1996
Goldberger, Paul, "Two on Base,
One Out in Toronto,"
The New York Times,
October 25, 1992
Harbison, Robert, *Creatures from
the Mind of the Engineer,
The Architecture of Santiago
Calatrava,* Artemis, Zurich, 1992
Hashimshony, Rifca, *Santiago
Calatrava. Structures and Movement,*
Exhibition catalogue, Haifa, 1997

Jodidio, Philip, *Oriente Station,*
Centralivros Lda., Lisbon, 1998
Ledbetter, James A., *Santiago
Calatrava. Structures in Movement.*
Exhibition catalogue, South China
Printing Company, Hong Kong 2001
Levin, Michael, *Calatrava. Drawings
and Sculptures.* Wolfau-Druck Rudolf
Mühlemann, Weinfelden, 2000
McQuaid, Matilda, *Santiago
Calatrava, Structure and Expression,*
The Museum of Modern Art,
New York, 1993
Molinari, Luca, *Santiago Calatrava,*
Exhibition catalogue, Skira, Milano,
1998
Nervi, Pier Luigi, *Aesthetics and
Technology in Building,
The Charles Eliot Norton Lectures,
1961-1962,* Harvard University
Press, Cambridge,
Massachusetts, 1965
Polano, Sergio, *Santiago Calatrava,
Complete Works,*
Ginkgo, Electa, Milan, 1996
Santiago Calatrava, 1983-93,
Catalogo de la exposición
antológica en la Lonja de Valencia
del 31 de Mayo al 30
de Junio de 1993, El Croquis
Editorial, Madrid, 1993
Sharp, Dennis (editor),
Santiago Calatrava, Architectural
Monographs n° 46, Academy
Editions, London, 1996
Tischhauser, Anthony, and
Stanislaus von Moos, *Santiago
Calatrava. Public Buildings,*
Birkhäuser, Basel, 1998
Tzonis, Alexander, Liane Lefaivre,
*Movement, Structure
and the Work of Santiago Calatrava,*
Birkhäuser, Basel, Boston,
Berlin 1995
Tzonis, Alexander, *Santiago
Calatrava. The Poetics of Movement,*
Universe Publishing, New York, 1999

Biografia > Biografia

1951 (28.7.) Santiago Calatrava Valls born in Benimamet near Valencia, Spain.

1956-1968 Primary and secondary schooling in Valencia.

1968-1969 Attends art school in Valencia.

1969-1974 Studies architecture at "Escuela Técnica Superior de Arquitectura de Valencia" qualifying as an architect. Post-graduate course in urbanism.

1975-1979 Studies civil engineering at the Swiss Federal Institute of Technology (ETH), Zurich.

1979-1981 Doctorate of technical science of the ETH, Ph.D. thesis: "Concerning the Foldability of Spaceframes". Assistant in the Institute for Building Statics and Construction and in the Institute for Aerodynamics and Lightweight Construction at the ETH, Zurich.

1981 Architectural and engineering practice established in Zurich.

1985 Exhibition of sculptures, Jamileh Weber Gallery, Zurich.

1987 Member of the BSA (Union of Swiss Architects). "Auguste Perret UIA Prize" (Union Internationale d'Architectes), Paris. Member of the International Academy of Architecture. Participation in the Triennale di Milano. Exhibition, Museum of Architecture, Basel.

1988 Art prize of the city of Barcelona for the Bach de Roda Bridge. "Premio de la Asociación de la prensa" (Award of the Press Association), Valencia. "IABSE Prize" (International Association for Bridge and Structural Engineering). "FAD" Prize (Fomento de las Artes y el Diseño), Spain. "Fritz Schumacher Prize", for "Urbanism, Architecture, Engineering", Hamburg. Fazlur Rahman Khan International Fellowship for Architecture and Engineering.

1989 Travelling exhibition: New York, St. Louis, Chicago, Los Angeles, Toronto, Montreal, Helsinki. Second architectural and engineering practice established in Paris. Honorary Member of the BDA (Union of German Architects).

1990 "Médaille d'Argent de la Recherche et de la Technique", Fondation Académie d'Architecture 1970, Paris.

1991 European "Glulam Award" (Glued Laminated Timber Construction), Munich. Exhibition, Suomen Rakennustaiteen, Helsinki. "Award for Good Buildings 1991", Zurich, for Stadelhofen Railway Station. Retrospective, Museum of Design, Zurich.

1992 Member of the "Real Academia de Bellas Artes de San Carlos", Valencia. Member of the Europe Academy, Cologne. "Brunel Award" for Stadelhofen Railway Station. Gold Medal of the Institute of Structural Engineers, London. Retrospective, Dutch Institute for Architecture, Rotterdam. Retrospective, Royal Institute of British Architects, London. Retrospective, Arkitektur Museet, Stockholm.

1993 Exhibition, Deutsches Museum, Munich. Exhibition, Museum of Modern Art, New York. Honorary Member of the Royal Institute of British Architects, London. Retrospective, La Lontja Museum, Valencia. Exhibition, Overbeck Society, Lübeck. Retrospective, Gammel Doc, Copenhagen. Honorary doctorate, Polytechnic, Valencia. "Medalla de Honor al Fomento de la Invención", Fundación García Cabrerizo, Madrid. "The City of Toronto Urban Design Awards", BCE Place, Toronto.

1994 Exhibition, Bruton Street Gallery, London. Honorary doctorate, the University of Seville. Exhibition, Museum of Applied and Folk Arts, Moscow. "Creu Sant Jordi", Generalitat de Catalunya, Barcelona. Honorary doctorate of fine arts, Heriot-Watt University, Edinburgh. Exhibition, Ma Gallery, Tokyo. Exhibition, Arqueria de los Nuevos Ministerios, Madrid. Exhibition, Santa Cruz, Tenerife.

1995 Exhibition, Centro Cultural de Belem, Lisbon. Exhibition, Fondazione Angelo Masieri, Venice. Honorary doctorate of technical science, University of Salford, England. Exhibition, Navarra Museum, Pamplona.

1996 "Medalla de Oro al Mérito de las Bellas Artes", the Ministry of Culture, Granada. Exhibition, Bilbao. Exhibition, Museum of Design, Zurich. Exhibition, Padova. Exhibition, Vira Gambarogno, Ascona, Bellinzona. Honorary doctorate, University of Glasgow. Exhibition, Venice. Exhibition, St. Gall. Exhibition, Basel. Exhibition, Milwaukee. Exhibition, London.

1997 Honorary doctorate, Institute of technology, Delft. Exhibition, Haifa. "Europäischer Stahlbaupreis" for the Kronprinzen Bridge, Berlin. Art Prize from Louis Vuitton–Moct Hennessy, Paris. Honorary doctorate, the University of Milwaukee. "Master de Oro del Forum de Alta Direccion", Madrid.

1998 Member of "Les Arts et Lettres", Paris. Exhibition, Triennale, Milano. "Brunel Awards, Madrid – Station d'Oriente", Lisbon. Lecture series for the School of Architecture and Design at Massachusetts Institute of Technology, Boston. Lecture series, Architecture Department, ETH Zurich.

1999 Honorary doctorate, Università degli Studi di Cassino. "Principe de Asturias" Art Prize, Spain. Honorary doctorate, University of Lund. "Foreign Member of the Academy", Royal Swedish Academy of Engineering Sciences, IVA. "Grau Grande Oficial da Ordem do Mérito", Chancelaria das Ordens Honorificas Portuguesas, Lisbon. "Gold Medal", The Concrete Society, London. Honourable Mention, "Canadian Consulting Engineering Awards" for the Mimico Creek Bridge, Toronto.

2000 Honorary doctorate, Universita degli Studi di Ferrara. Traveling Exhibition, Montevideo and Buenos Aires. Honorary Fellowship, Royal Architectural Institute of Canada College of Fellows. "Das Goldene Dach 2000", structural completion of the "Pfalzkeller", St. Gallen. Fellowship, Institute for Urban Design, New York, N.Y. Honorary Fellowship, National Academy of Architecture, Monterrey, N.L. Lecture series for the School of Architecture and Design at Massachusetts Institute of Technology, Boston. Guest of Honour, Mexico City, D.F. Government. Exhibition, Palazzo Strozzi, Florence. Exhibition, The IVA Royal Technology Forum, Stockholm. "Algur H. Meadows Award for Excellence in the Arts", Meadows School of Arts, Dallas. "Medalla de Oro, Círculo de Bellas Artes", Valencia. Honorary Academician, Real Academia de Bellas Artes de San Fernando, Madrid.

2001 Prize „Exitos 2000" to the best architectonical work, Museo de las Ciencias, Valencia. Exhibition, National Gallery, Alexandro Soutzos Museum, Athens. Exhibition, Meadows Museum, Southern Methodist University, Dallas. Prize „Award for Excellence in Design" for the Times Capsule, American Museum of Natural History, New York. Exhibition at the IVAM Centre Julio González, Valencia.